RAILS OF WAR

STEVEN JAMES HANTZIS

RAILS OF WAR

SUPPLYING THE AMERICANS AND THEIR ALLIES IN CHINA-BURMA-INDIA

Potomac Books

AN IMPRINT OF THE UNIVERSITY OF NEBRASKA PRESS

All rights reserved. Potomac Books is an imprint of the
University of Nebraska Press.
Manufactured in the United States of America.

Library of Congress Control Number: 2017932331
Set in Lyon Text by Rachel Gould.

Contents

Illustrations

Preface

This book is a personal exploration of the unsung China-Burma-India theater of World War II. My father, James Harry Hantzis, left behind a cardboard box of military keepsakes, a Madonna-and-child cameo ring that my wife now wears, and a captivating photo scrapbook entitled *India*. And he left behind father-and-son stories.

I guess it's natural for little boys to be fascinated with the military and to act out battles with fabricated weapons and imaginary consequences. At least it was normal where I grew up. A boy's imagination could be stimulated into militaristic overdrive with television shows like *The Big Picture* and Hollywood movies like *The Bridge on the River Kwai* and *To Hell and Back*, as was mine. I was lucky to have a younger brother I could enlist as a comrade or target as an enemy, depending on how our imaginations percolated on any given day. We attacked strongholds, propelled lethal objects at enemy positions, and built forts in our barn's haymow complete with booby traps and secret passages. It was good, clean fun. We were boys just trying to be like the men of my father's generation.

I've used the real names of men who served, men I felt I knew well enough to attempt to write in their voices, but their words are mine. There are no recordings of their conversations, so with the details I had at hand I took authorial license and wrote the dialogue. The stories and situations, the vignettes, are real.

From each monochrome kernel of truth I have attempted to grow colorful, dense flora to appeal to the mind's eye. But my humble apology must now be offered in advance. After working on the railroad for twelve years, then in the American labor movement for thirty, and after befriending the good men who served in the 721st Railway Operating Battalion and hearing their accounts firsthand, I confess with assurance that even my most imaginative and crafty passages, those snippets where I manage to conjure vivid flashes and move along the narrative, are most certainly pale and poky compared to what really happened.

The story begins this way: In the generation before mine there were men of substance and courage, wisdom and wile who moved the weight of war on ribbons of steel. At this, the work of their lives, they were better than anyone, anywhere.

Acknowledgments

A stone inscribed with the words *China-Burma-India* rests at the southern end of the National World War II Memorial on the National Mall in Washington DC, just a few miles from my home in Alexandria, Virginia. The marker is one in a constellation of stones presided over by the vaulted arch of the Pacific Pavilion rising to commemorate one of two great theaters in the global mêlée. Many believe the stone is not grand enough to evoke all that China-Burma-India meant to the war effort. The stone symbolizes a subaltern war often declared "the forgotten theater" by historians as well as the men who served. I'm thankful that not everyone has forgotten.

My father, James Harry Hantzis, inspired this book and provided not only stories but also a collection of black-and-white photographs titled simply *India*. His life was an unconscious example of the character of his generation and a model that I will forever strive to fulfill. He is long gone. But some of the men with whom he served in the 721st Railway Operating Battalion are still alive. Until just a few years ago they held a reunion every September in upstate New York. There, in 2002, I met Don Blair, E. O. Woods, George Lee, William Butler, Charles Graham, Lyle Sanderson, William Walsh, and Herb Witt. All of these men contributed not just stories and inspiration but artifacts and photographs, especially the engaging motorman E. O. Woods, president of the Reunion Committee.

But I never would have met these fine men and many others had it not been for the sparkplug of the battalion, the locomotive fireman Rocky Agrusti. Rocky is that rare, honor-bound individual who unabashedly holds dear his service to his country and that of his family as well as all who wore the uniform. Rocky kindly introduced me to his extensive network of friends and comrades and provided a personal tour of his "museum," a capacious collection of military items housed in a former sawmill on his lovely property in New York.

Rocky's late-evening phone calls always served as a motivator when my writing seemed to lag. My wife, Kathleen, and I were honored to accompany him to the final roundup of the national CBI World War II Veterans Association on the sixtieth anniversary of the end of the war. Rocky's lively cohort of seven hundred veterans, their spouses and families, were an inspiration. Many, Rocky among them, had more energy and love of life than the generation thirty years their juniors.

It was during a tour of the National World War II Memorial and Arlington Cemetery that Rocky revealed a salient truth of his generation. I had noticed that once the veterans observed their man-made surroundings, they turned their backs to the construction, formed small groups, and talked to each other almost oblivious to the monuments. Unusual, I thought; after all, the monuments were built to honor their accomplishments and bravery. When I asked Rocky about this he answered without hesitation, "It's really all about the fellowship."

There are two more members of the battalion who deserve special mention, both men I have yet to meet face to face. The first is Stewart White, who was a good friend of my father and has shared with me touching letters and photographs. The other is Alvin Carder, a Company B locomotive machinist who worked in the same shop as my dad. Alvin provided a colorful enlisted man's history and is a fifty-year member of my father's union and my employer, the International Association of Machinists and Aerospace Workers.

I also greatly appreciated Tom Foltz's correspondence, reminiscences, and photographs. Tom served with the 789th Pipeliners Battalion stationed at Parbatipur and played the trumpet in the acclaimed camp orchestra.

My immediate family deserves thanks on many levels. My wife patiently lived with this project and its demands for fifteen years. Kathleen was my ever-ready traveling partner, critic, and intellectual sounding board. My daughter, Sara, and her husband, Pat McSparin, both with firm literary grounding, provided instant editorial support. To my bright young nephew, Patrick, I owe appreciation for never failing to prompt me about the book's progress at our frequent family get-togethers. And I owe a special debt of gratitude to my wife's mother, Mary Flaherty, who volunteered to be the first to read the vast unedited narrative and provided assistive comments, corrections, and encouragement. Most recently my gratitude goes to Jefferson Morley, who bravely confronted my 350,000-word draft and with the precision of a surgeon carved the steak from the beast.

RAILS OF WAR

1

ss *Mariposa*

The bow of the ship plowed through the blue-green Pacific with a mesmerizing determination. The men of the 721st Railway Operating Battalion were one day at sea, roughly 500 miles southwest of Los Angeles, and what worried them most were their guts.

The food was horrible. The sea was nauseating. Their quarters were cramped and the distractions few. Some men were violently ill, and more were queasy. To all, life had lost its charm. Only a lucky few seemed immune to the bow's plunge, the stern's lift, and then the wallowing roll. The cycle endlessly repeated without mercy, without a horizon to anchor the mind or an end in sight to soothe the soul.

To further confound the senses the ship zigzagged across the chop, changing direction unpredictably every few miles, as the captain maneuvered to throw off Japanese submarines. The thinking was that it takes an enemy submarine eight minutes to target and fire a spread of torpedoes, so the *Mariposa* changed course abruptly every six minutes.[1] Everywhere the men looked their fellow soldiers were covering their mouths and rushing down halls or to the railings. "Railbirds," they were called.

Their first meal on ship was a bad omen. Each man received a card with a large black letter printed on it: A, B, C, or D. When the ship's loudspeakers, hung in every corridor and deck, boomed, "All men holding B cards proceed to the midship stairway," off went the Bs.

After an hour's wait in line, what they found disgusted them. Some men, after sweating out the chow line, got a whiff of the food and bolted for the nearest place to get sick again. Breakfast was grease-soaked soybean sausages and salted mackerel. The only things edible were the bread and potatoes.

The fare seemed like a cruel joke compared with the fare at Camp Atterbury in Indiana, where they had mustered before taking a train to California. To add gratuitous insult to their culinary injuries, there were only to be two meals a day. Upon reflection the men couldn't decide if this was a good thing or a bad thing.

The situation went from disgusting to debilitating on the second day, when even the bread, now infested with mealy bugs, was inedible. Seeing no action after complaining up the chain of command, the men resorted to a tactic from civilian life: they went on strike. The culture of direct action, a common feature of their railroad employment, was alive and well even after a year of army discipline and top-down conditioning.

The men refused to eat, not the greatest hardship, or take part in the fire and lifeboat drills and physical training, a rather bigger problem for their superiors. With mutiny in the air an armed marine guard was posted for meals.[2]

The strike didn't last long. The officers and noncoms on board had the same concerns. No one was court-martialed or disciplined, and the food got better. But it would never reach the high standards set stateside, and as the men settled into a shipboard routine they grumbled all the way.

...

At 18,017 gross tons, the SS *Mariposa* was a large ship for her day. Designed by Gibbs and Cox, Inc. and built by the Bethlehem Shipbuilding Corporation in Quincy, Massachusetts, she was launched for the Matson Navigation Company in Los Angeles in July 1931. She was laid out to accommodate 475 first-class and 229 cabin class passengers along with 359 crew members. On this trip she carried five times as many passengers. The *Mariposa* was the floating home—and potential Japanese target—for nearly 5,000 souls, including the 651 enlisted men, 21 officers, and 1 warrant officer of the 721st Railway Operating Battalion, a unit sponsored by the New York Central Railroad.

The men of the 721st weren't the only railroaders on board. They shared quarters with the 725th Railway Operating Battalion, which consisted of men who had been working the Chicago, Rock Island and Pacific Railroad; the 726th, an outfit sponsored by the Wabash Railroad; the 745th, from the Chicago, Burlington & Quincy Railroad; the 748th, associated with the Texas & Pacific Railroad; and the 758th, a railway shop battalion from Ohio. Also on board were the 705th Infantry Replacement Battalion, forty civilian engineers, ten nurses, a headquarters staff, a hospital staff, and even some civilian passengers, in addition to the Merchant Marine crew and the Navy Armed Guard.

In preparation for their mission, the men of the 721st had trained for five months at Camp Cushing in the blistering sun of south Texas, studying the nomenclature of weapons and drilling with gas masks before going on to technical training. Most of the men in the battalion had railroad experience, but some didn't. The men with no mechanical experience were given crash courses on operating lathes, shapers, drill presses, and grinders under the tutelage of the Southern Pacific supervisors. Men with no experience operating locomotives and switching cars were bombarded with the golden rule of the industry: *There are no small accidents on the railroad! Work safe! Take your time and do things right!*

The shop crafts repaired air brakes, worked in drop pits, set valves, washed out boilers, ran water tests, lubricated everything in sight, and packed journal boxes. The car repair platoon worked on wheel trucks and couplers and replaced brass bushings on axle journals. The wreck crew worked with the steam crane and rerailed wayward equipment. The operating crafts switched cars, kicked cuts into sidings, learned to work a manifest, and practiced driving doubleheaders—two engines and tenders coupled together.

After their training was complete, they shipped out, first to Camp Atterbury and then to the final staging area at Camp Anza in the southern California desert. When they arrived at the dock in Long Beach, heads swiveled as the awestruck young men from the Midwest and other inland states catalogued their strange new surroundings: the squawking, insistent gulls, buoys gonging in the harbor, and the smell of salt water. It was the first time most of the men had seen oceangoing vessels and the massive equipment

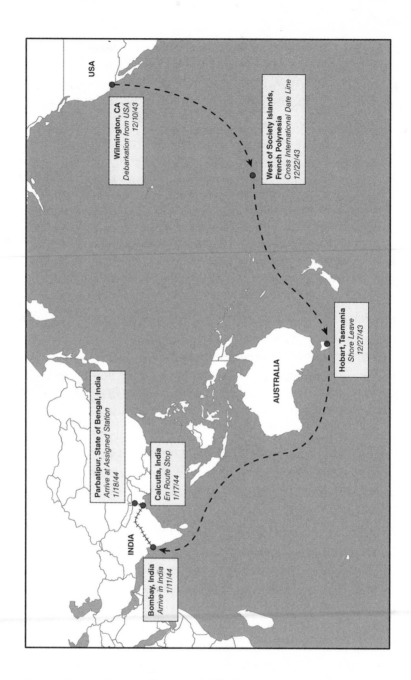

MAP 1. Route of 721st Railway Operating Battalion (ROB) from the United States to its assigned station, Parbatipur, State of Bengal, India, December 10, 1943–January 18, 1944. Map by Erin Greb.

needed for their maintenance close enough to touch. These were men who, for the most part, were familiar with large industrial settings and oversized equipment, but this was something new. "My God," more than one of them thought, "these things are enormous!"

Now they were sailing into harm's way. The *Mariposa* was lightly armed. She carried a five-inch 38-caliber gun on the stern and a three-inch 50-caliber gun on the bow. Along her steering station were two three-inch 50-caliber guns, and she sported two Swiss-designed 20mm Oerlikon anti-aircraft guns on the foredeck and two more on the afterdeck. All the weapons were in raised gun tubs except for the four 20mm guns on the flying bridge. The fighting capabilities of the *Mariposa* were purely defensive. Should she find herself in contact with an enemy surface ship or submarine her standing orders were to turn away, put the attacker on the stern, and flee.

The *Mariposa* was sailing solo because the United States and Britain had taken a page from their World War I playbooks, where they learned it was less risky to transport soldiers on big, fast luxury liners than on slow troop carriers escorted by battleships. In August 1942 the two countries began using the French SS *Pasteur*, the Canadian *Empress of Scotland*, and the Cunard Queens, both *Mary* and *Elizabeth*, to move men across the seas.

. . .

Each day grew hotter as the *Mariposa* tacked southward. The men diverted themselves with board games: Chinese checkers, backgammon, Cavalcade, Horse Races (no betting), and Monopoly, as well as cribbage boards, cards (both regular and pinochle), card games (Pit and Rook), jigsaw puzzles, chess, checkers, and dominoes. A competent band was organized to serenade the passengers. Upon crossing the equator an ad hoc theatrical troupe put on a production of *The Court of Old King Neptune*, complete with a queen whose elbow-length blond hair displayed the versatile uses of a mop and whose faint falsetto voice registered with a pronounced New Jersey accent.

The journey south was also a journey west. Every day the men turned back their watches as time zones passed invisibly. The weather turned chilly, and the men wore their field jackets on deck. Then, just west of the Society Islands of French Polynesia, December 23 disappeared entirely. Calendars and diaries jumped forward from December 22 to December 24.[3]

. . .

When Christmas Day dawned, Jim Hantzis didn't feel well, and it had nothing to do with the ship ride or the bad food. They had been fourteen days at sea, and it seemed like a lifetime since he had seen his wife, Marilou. Six months before, Hantzis had wangled a five-day pass from Camp Cushing and taken a train to Indianapolis for their wedding in the Zion Evangelical United Church of Christ. At the altar, with Reverend F. R. Daries conducting the ceremony, Jim wore his dress uniform and Marilou wore a light blue suit with a single strand of pearls, earrings to match, and a red rose corsage. Their hands found each other, and they hung on for dear life. They had been dating for over two years and their familiarity was now their security.

The night before, Jim and Marilou had partied with their friends at the Westlake Dance Club. Now, at their modest wedding reception, these same friends mingled with family members, the young couple danced to Tony Martin singing "Tonight We Love," and Marilou drank blackberry wine.[4] In the morning, after the couple spent the night at the Hantzis house, Jim's mother greeted the late-rising Marilou with "Good morning, bride!" Then Jim headed back to Camp Cushing. Except for a brief rendezvous in November, when he was stationed at Camp Atterbury, he and Marilou did not see each other again before he sailed off.

In the privacy of his stateroom Jim took off his wedding ring and in the dim light tried to make out its simple inscription, *MLH & JHH 6/13/43*. Thoughts of his wedding day helped lift his mood, but there wasn't a lot the *Mariposa* could offer for Christmas cheer. The men got some turkey with their second meal and savored their portions as they shuffled along in the aluminum room. And of course the company clowns fashioned Santa hats from socks and decorated the corridors with cardboard cutouts of Rudolph posed in a variety of traditional and not-so-traditional acts.

Two days later the ship docked at Hobart, Tasmania, beneath the snow-capped peak of Mount Wellington, and the men got a brief shore leave. But less than thirty-six hours later the stout mooring lines holding the *Mariposa* in port were cast to the dock, where they landed with a thud. The same dull release was felt in the hearts of her departing visitors. As her powerful turbines settled into their familiar drone, the ship's forward assembly area filled with officers and noncoms. They were finally going to hear from the brass about where they were going.

All the rail battalions received their orders in turn, and the 721st, being the lowest numbered battalion, heard first. Their destination was a place they had never heard of: the city of Parbatipur in the State of Bengal, India. They would disembark in fourteen days at Bombay, on the other side of the subcontinent.

The sergeants, who received a further, technical briefing involving area maps, terrain analysis, logistical details, and cultural specifics, then went to the enlisted men with what they had been told. The briefing of a squad in Company B went like this:

SERGEANT HANTZIS: (Reading from his clipboard.) In fourteen days, with the cooperation of the Imperial Japanese Navy, we will debark at the port of Bombay, India, and proceed by rail with our equipment to Parbatipur in the State of Bengal. There we will establish a camp and conduct railroad operations, without the aid of modern block control or classification yard systems, over approximately 120 miles of single-line main. The other battalions will operate to the east with a final terminus at Ledo.

Ledo is the end of the line, and it straddles the India-Burma border. It is currently under the protection of the British, American, and Chinese armies.

From Ledo the supplies that we transport will be flown by aircraft over the Himalayan Mountains to British and American special operation forces in Burma and China as well as regular army units of the Kuomintang. Eventually, when the Ledo road is complete, these supplies will be trucked from Ledo to China.

The railroads we will operate are of three different gauges: broad gauge, narrow gauge, and metre gauge. The terrain is hilly to mountainous, with swamps and numerous bridged waterways. One water passage will be by ferry.

The native workforce is composed of Indian Hindus of various castes and Mohammedan laborers. The Hindus and Mohammedans dislike each other, and the Hindus won't speak to someone not in their caste.

There are no municipal amenities such as running water or sewage treatment. Disease will be a constant threat, and personal vigilance will be necessary to avoid inflection from typhus, malaria, and dysentery. There are numerous poisonous insects and reptiles and reports of Japanese sympathizers among the Indian independence movement. This movement is particularly strong in the State of Bengal.

Any questions?

WISENHEIMER # 1: Sarge, is this were the tigers live?

(Chuckles in the squad.)

SERGEANT: Yes, and don't pet 'em.

(Laughter all around.)

WISENHEIMER # 2: What's a Mohammedan?

SERGEANT: Someone who believes in a religion different than yours. It's their country and their religion. Treat them with respect.

(Silent acceptance.)

WISENHEIMER # 3: Will we get to see the Taj Mahal?

SERGEANT: You'll be lucky to see a pool hall.

(Some laughs, some moans, and a plaintive whine of "Ah, Sarge, come on.")

SERGEANT: You will familiarize yourselves with this document from the War Department. (He holds up a brown four-by-five-inch booklet from the War and Navy Departments, *A Pocket Guide to India*.) This booklet will allow you to fit in and respect the native culture. I emphasize: *Respect the native culture.*

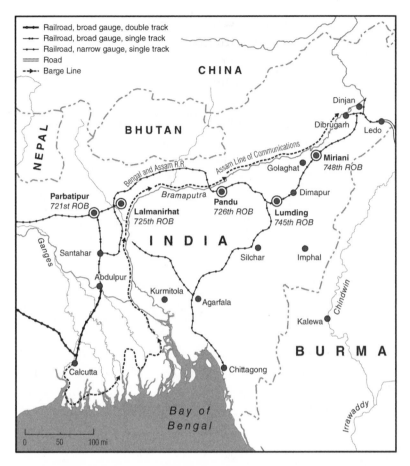

MAP 2. U.S. Army Railway Operating Battalions, Bengal and Assam Railway, March 1944. West to east: 721st, Parbatipur; 725th, Lalmanirhat; 726th, Pandu; 745th, Lumding; and, 748th, Miriani. Map by Erin Greb.

In addition to this document you are expected to listen to the Hindustani language lessons that will be broadcast on the ship's PA and make a conscientious effort to learn phrases and words that will facilitate your communication with the native population.

WISENHEIMER # 4: Some of dees guys from Brooklyn need to learn English before they can tackle Hindu-whatever.

(Chuckles all around.)

(From the back of the squad comes a defensive, high-pitched voice: "Yaaa! Well some of yooze hicks couldn't recognize a sophisticated linguist if he up and popped you in the schnozola.")

(Chorus of laughter from the rest of the men.)

SERGEANT: Fight the enemy, not each other. And one more thing: we couldn't take on as much fresh water as we planned to in Hobart. Therefore we're placing guards on the water taps and expect that no fresh water will be wasted from here to India.

Finally, the ship's captain has asked that all you guys who are pounding your British coins into souvenir rings remember that a sound like that carries through the water like a telegraph, and unless you want to make the Japs' job of sinking us easier, knock it off!

(Silent acceptance.)

SERGEANT: That is all. Don't forget to sign up for water guard duty. Now get to work.

When the joking subsided reality sank in. The American soldier railroaders were going to build, rebuild, and operate the rail infrastructure that would supply Allied forces fighting to oust the Imperial Japanese Army from the China-Burma-India theater. It was, said Gen. Brehon Burke Somervell, commander of the Army Service Forces, "the greatest engineering undertaking of the War."[5]

2

Leaving Bombay

On January 13, 1944, after thirty days at sea, the men of the 721st Railway Operating Battalion finished their stopover in Bombay. They had enjoyed two days of leave in the city of two million people, guided mostly by their wits and copies of *A Pocket Guide to India*. They saw the Taj Mahal Hotel, rode in rickshaws, sampled the *pani-puri chat* (fried noodles and vegetables), avoided the red-light district, and visited the Hanging Gardens overlooking the sea.

Now the British were in charge of transportation. If the Yanks had any notion of traveling in Oriental splendor to their ultimate destination, the Bengali city of Parbatipur, it was quickly put to rest. As the men of the 721st saw their train waiting at the pier in Bombay, they couldn't believe it was meant for passenger service. It was broad gauge—five foot, six inches rail to rail—and unattended. Most of the men thought it was a livestock number. The wooden cars were dilapidated and dingy. As the men were assigned compartments some hopefully muttered that the decrepit coaches must be temporary accommodations, but no such luck befell these optimists; these cars were their billets for the next five days.

The Indian railway service considered the rundown coaches to be third-class accommodations. The men of the 721st did not rate them so highly. The painted walls were worn to the wood from the multitudes crowding aboard. Rough timber benches ran the length of the cars; they were painful to sit on, and the men were supposed to sleep on them as well. Thankfully the cracked and broken windows opened to dissipate the stench from the rotting tea, fruit, and *paan* spit. Roaches, rats, and mice were the churlish hosts into whose home the men had wandered, and mosquitoes saw to it that nobody rested for long.

Then the men waited . . . and waited some more.

It was early evening before the locomotive's shrill whistle blew and the Yanks got their first jolt of movement. The men of the 721st were unceremoniously seen off by grousing beggars, blind people guided by children, and gauze-covered lepers. Unlike their send-off at Long Beach there were no bands, no flags, no banners, and no cute Red Cross volunteers handing out sandwiches and fresh coffee. The moment was inauspicious but very Indian.

Darkness came over the train shortly after crossing the Ulhas River into the outskirts of Bombay. Somewhere before Shahapur the men began to bunk down as best they could. The night was cool and the train's movement helped to keep the air fresh, but there was no comfort to be had. If the men slept at all it was between bug bites, whistle blasts, and washed-out rail beds. The wheels on the coaches hadn't been machined regularly, if ever, and their flat spots added an out-of-rhythm *thunk* to the prosaic *clickety-clack*.

They were drawing ever closer to the war zone.

. . .

At the time, the Japanese Armed Forces held the upper hand in the China-Burma-India theater. They had been on a strategic offensive across Asia since their 1931 invasion of Manchuria. Now, in early 1944, they occupied all of China's major cities and much of her rice-producing areas and, with the conquest of Burma only five months after Pearl Harbor, controlled all of China's deepwater ports and logistical supply routes.

The Allies believed control of China was the key to winning the war in the Pacific. The Americans began supplying China in April 1941, when President Franklin D. Roosevelt approved lend-lease aid. Shortly after, fighter planes, spare parts, and gasoline began arriving via the Port of Rangoon, then moving by rail to Lashio and on up the Burma Road to Yunnan Province in China.[1] But in May 1942 that route was taken from them.

The Allies looked at China as a land-based aircraft carrier from which to bomb the Japanese home islands and ultimately launch an invasion from Korea. That was the plan in January 1944, when the 721st arrived in India. The secret of the atomic bomb was still locked away in the deserts of New Mexico.

Questions abounded. How could the Allies supply the Chinese Nationalist Army under Generalissimo Chiang Kai-shek—a less than enthusiastic ally—and keep him from switching sides? After all, if Chiang switched sides it would be a double-edged sword, freeing up two million seasoned Japanese soldiers to fight elsewhere and allowing the generalissimo's forces, ineffective though they may be, to threaten the Allies in Burma and India.[2] But more to the point, how could the Allies hold on to India, the base from which the resupply of China was to be accomplished?

Two problems, one solution: logistics. The United States could produce the needed matériel, but getting it to the front would be daunting. So long as the Allies controlled eastern India and the provinces of Bengal and Assam, they could move freight from Calcutta's deepwater port on the Hooghly River via the less than optimized Indian railroads to their supply depot at Ledo. That was a starting point. But control of India was not a given. The British and Americans had been run out of Burma in May 1942 and were still on their proverbial heels. The rising Indian independence movement made for shifting political ground that undermined British authority and prompted rearguard attacks and sabotage. The impact of Japanese anticolonial propaganda—"Asia for the Asians"—was measurable and unsettling. Surrendering Indian troops captured in Malaya and Singapore organized into a Japanese combat division of 40,000 men. The Azad Hind Fauj (Indian National Army) under the leadership of Subhas Chandra Bose, a Bengali independence leader, threw in their lot with the Japanese and Germans. They hoped the Axis powers would kick the British out of India.

Militarily the Japanese were on the move as well. In late December 1943 Gen. Mutaguchi Renya and his Eighteenth Division, now firmly in charge of Burma, had begun Operation U-Go and were bringing to bear 150,000 hardened jungle fighters against the big British base at Imphal and its vulnerable supply line. Mutaguchi had clobbered the British in every encounter from Singapore to

Burma. Now the mercurial general wanted Imphal as a birthday gift for his emperor.

The Allies' logistical problems simply could not be solved using the existing infrastructure. The lazy Bengal and Assam Railroad, which normally serviced tea plantations, wasn't up to speed, and the Allies couldn't airlift enough supplies to the Chinese. "Flying the Hump"—crossing the prohibitive Himalayas between China and Burma—was a dangerous and courageous affair. The humble twin-engine Douglas DC-47 aircraft was a workhorse but carried less than three tons of matériel on each perilous trip, while Chiang Kai-shek had between two and three million Nationalist troops under his loose command.[3] What the Allies needed was an overland route of nearly 1,200 miles to run truck convoys from India to China.[4] That road, the Ledo Road, had yet to be built.

These two problems, the railroad and the jungle road, would be solved by Americans. First, the Americans decided to build a "combat roadway" from the Indian border town of Ledo through the jungles and mountains of Japanese-occupied Burma into China. That job was assigned to primarily African American construction units led by white officers. The movement of thousands of tons of war matériel over dilapidated, poorly repaired, nonconcurrent Indian railways fell to the men of the 721st and the other railroad battalions. All told, the Allied supply line would run 14,000 miles from the West Coast ports of the United States, through the teaming docks of Calcutta, to the city of Chongqing in China. It was an ambitious plan indeed.

In January 1944 the men of the 721st Railway Operating Battalion entrained in a strange new country on a strange new railroad to begin an inconceivable adventure with life-and-death consequences. Their future was unknown, and their motivation and skills would be profoundly tested over the coming twenty months.

3

Indian Rails

Indian railways were an outgrowth of colonial necessity. Their dual purpose was to expand commerce and make certain that British troops had quick transport to quell rebellions in remote corners of the subcontinent. Of course it didn't take long for wily insurgents to learn to blow up the tracks *before* rebelling.

The politics of building a railroad in India were much debated in Britain a century earlier. In the 1850s a split developed between those who thought the Indian population should be pacified first and those who believed building the railroad system would accomplish that goal. This history, while unknown to the American railroad men, would shape their experience in the China-Burma-India theater.

Strikes on Indian railroads were as old as the system itself. In 1854 the first train in eastern India ran from Howrah, Calcutta's sister city on the western bank of the Hooghly River, to Pandua, a distance of twenty-four miles. By 1862 the workers had organized and become motivated to strike Howrah Station. There, 1,200 strong, they demanded an eight-hour working day. The peak of labor militancy would come eighty-four years later, a few months after the departure of the 721st, when Indian railroad workers aligned with the independence movement to force the British out.[1]

. . .

Indian railroads were an instrument of British power. An article in the October 10, 1857, issue of *Railway Times* argued the conservative *pacify first* position:

> In the first place, the whole peninsula must be tranquillised and an assurance fixed upon the English mind that the peace of Hindostan

shall not again be disturbed. Until this essential preliminary is established, not a mortgage upon the whole revenues derived under the charter is likely to induce English capital and labour to embark for settlement or operation in India. This sense of security is not to be obtained by a mere chastisement of the mutineers. Our suspicions lead us to imagine that chastisement must follow nearer home. If fear is to be irrevocably impressed upon the native mind, the whole of the civil and military establishments, which the mutineers have treated with contempt must be removed. Not merely the men but the system must be changed. Neither Hindoo nor Mussulman must be permitted to imagine that he can repeat his effort a second time.... When such a plan of government is set afoot ... then may British rule and modern civilisation consider themselves on the pathway of security. Then also, and not till then, may an extension of the railway system be profitably introduced into what are still the barbaric lands of Inde.[2]

The passion and sanctimony of the *pacify first* faction notwithstanding, the *railroad first* supporters carried the day. Construction plans went forward after industrial, shipping, and commercial interests prevailed upon the British Parliament to guarantee a 5 percent rate of return on investment as an incentive for capitalists to build Indian railroads.

With this sticky wicket resolved, financial arrangements began in earnest for what would be the largest infrastructure investment ever by any colonial power. Conquering the subcontinent with investment largesse did not, however, always go smoothly. Another article from *Railway Times,* a May 1859 issue, tells the sad story of just how brutal railroading was on the forerunner of the Bengal and Assam line, the railroad the 721st would operate:

East Indian—Slaughter of Mr. Evans

It is with the deepest sorrow we have to announce the murder of Mr. William Evans, the chief engineer of the Jubbulpore branch of the East Indian. Mr. Evans was out in the district with his staff ... running out the centre line for the Jubbulpore Railway. They had a small guard of forty-eight Seikhs, supplied by the Government of India....

It appears that on the morning of 26th March, while the guards were cooking their food, the encampment was suddenly surprised by about a thousand rebels; the Seikhs, though half undressed, flew to their arms, and the engineers jumped on their horses. Mr. Evans, it appears, became perfectly bewildered: the havildar [sergeant] of the guard said to him that if he would clear his front, his men would commence firing upon the rebels, but Mr. Evans waved his hand in the negative, and the engineers then fled in different directions. Mr. Evans and Mr. Limnell's horses became restive with the firing, and rearing, threw their riders. While Mr. Evans was lying on the ground, the rebels came up, speared him first and beheaded him afterwards.[3]

But the British are nothing if not persistent. By March 1870 they had designed and financed, and the Indians had built, a rail line between Bombay and Calcutta. Two years later the Frenchman Jules Verne wrote about the ever-so-English Phileas Fogg and his servant, Passepartout, traveling around the world having wagered 20,000 pounds that they could make it in eighty days. Part of their journey took them through India on the new British railway. The supremely confident Fogg tells us:

Formerly one was obliged to travel in India by the old cumbrous methods of going on foot or on horseback, in palanquins or unwieldy coaches; now fast steamboats ply on the Indus and the Ganges, and a great railway, with branch lines joining the main line at many points on its route, traverses the peninsula from Bombay to Calcutta in three days. This railway does not run in a direct line across India. The distance between Bombay and Calcutta, as the bird flies, is only from one thousand to eleven hundred miles; but the deflections of the road increase this distance by more than a third.[4]

The men of the 721st were now making the same Bombay-to-Calcutta transit as the adventurous Mr. Fogg, only without faithful if somewhat addled servants like Passepartout. Admiration for the relative progress in transport was also missing.

By 1944, when the 721st arrived, the railroads of India provided strategic lines of communication for passengers, goods, and troops. The economy and national defense depended squarely on its service. Its 43,000 miles formed a commercial backbone connecting the ports of Bombay and Calcutta to every major moneymaking region and population center.[5] The system was a source of nationalistic pride and an important political symbol to the burgeoning Indian independence movement. Its workforce, courted by independence activists because of their economic leverage, was agitated and unafraid of direct action.

In January 1944 the Indian railway system, still the largest employer in the country, was in disrepair. Shortages during the First World War had caused the railroad to be cannibalized for parts. Repair shops had been converted to munitions factories and equipment went without maintenance. By the time the 721st arrived unreliable locomotives pulled ill-maintained equipment over unimproved rail beds of three incompatible gauges. This rundown system was operated by an Indian workforce that was political, pro-independence, divided by religion and caste, and, to be polite, not all that motivated. Some in the workforce, as the Americans would soon discover, had opposing sympathies and were capable saboteurs.

The mission of the 721st, and all the railroaders in CBI, was to work with the Indians and British, politely take charge of their railroad, and move lots of freight to the Burma-China front as quickly as possible, preferably yesterday. To accomplish their mission the men would need the skills of politicians, diplomats, anthropologists, linguists, and industrial engineers as well as those of their railroad crafts. And as they tried day after day to subsist on British rations they discovered another valuable and necessary skill: philosophical detachment.

The first two days of their journey took them through steep grades and valleys where the harvesting of bamboo sustained the local economy. Lean men working with long knives and handsaws looked up at the passing train with suspicious eyes as they rendered their commodity ready for transport on indifferent oxen and elephants. As the hills slowly leveled, the train passed through a swamp where the insects swarmed as thick as fog. The men of the 721st were curious aliens and transitory spectators watching and cataloguing the malarial landscape unfolding before them. The swamp at last gave way to more arid land as the soldiers arrived on the brim of the breadbasket, or, more correctly, the rice bowl of India. For miles on end their rolling picture show presented a scene with only slight variation.

Indian men and women tended small paddies, sometimes only forty feet square, demarked by earthen dams rising barely a foot above the languid pools. Rain provided the water and the Indians the seedling plants. The rest was a matter of time and fortune. These tiny squares of subsistence and sustenance, *amans*, were the architecture of India's soul. When these social building blocks tumbled, so did the people. The fate of rice was the fate of all. When rice was scarce people perished by the hundreds of thousands—even millions—their fortunes conjoined with the vagaries of nature as well as the ambition of man.

Rice began nurturing the soul of India 7,000 years before Christ was born. Seven centuries after that, farmers along the Brahmaputra Valley in Bengal and Assam constructed irrigation systems to support its cultivation.[6] So woven together were the fates of the crop and those who farmed it that the ancient Tamil saint Auvaiyar, the gifted female poet devotee of Ganesha, the Lord of Success, spelled it out in aphoristic verse in the eighth century:

When the rice-bunds are high, the irrigation water will rise;
When the water rises, the paddy will grow;
When the paddy grows, the inhabitants will thrive;
When the inhabitants thrive, the kingdom will flourish;
When the kingdom flourishes, the king will prosper.[7]

To these elegant lines the pessimist—and the student of Indian history—might add, "And vice versa."

The men of the 721st were about to encounter the antithesis of Auvaiyar's rosy representation. Their fateful journey would innocently deliver them into the midst of a terrible famine, the Panchasher Manvantar (Famine of Fifty, named for 1350, the Bengali year of its occurrence). Only a year before the arrival of the 721st, Indians in the State of Bengal had reached the point all peasants fear and dread: they began eating the seeds from which the coming year's crop was to be planted. Their predicament came at the confluence of man-made, state-made, and atmospheric disruptions, all rending the frail fabric of the natural order. To this catastrophe the 721st would arrive armed but without understanding or forewarning, though they could not have imagined its ghastly proportions had someone told them. The sated Americans had no point of reference for the scale of deprivation surrounding them. It would take time for the horror to sink in.

By the 1940s the British had converted Burma into the world's largest exporter of rice, and nearby Bengal, with sixty million Indians, had grown accustomed to receiving nearly 20 percent of its food from its eastern neighbor.[8] With the invasion of Burma and subsequent occupation by the Japanese, its surplus rice began flowing east, not west. At the same time the British introduced emergency measures in India and began to hoard stocks of grain for their military forces. In Chittagong, the region closest to Burma, the British instituted a scorched-earth policy to deny supplies to the Japanese and at the same time began exporting Indian rice to feed British troops in the Middle East and Ceylon.

Then, as the cataclysm took shape, in mid-October 1942 the entire east coast of Bengal and Orissa was wrecked by a furious cyclone. The destruction and flooding reached forty miles inland and wiped out the standing aman crop, which had been planted in June and July and was to be harvested starting later that month. Two months later the hand of man again intervened with martial ambition. During the week before Christmas Japanese air raids on Calcutta panicked the local population and collapsed the vulnerable food distribution network throughout eastern India. By May 1943 starving farmers had eaten their seed crop, wartime inflation had undermined any possibility of purchasing food, government corruption and inaction stalled meaningful relief policies, and the combination swept away nearly four million Bengali souls.[9] The peak in the death rate followed a year later, in December 1943, a month before the 721st arrived in India. As that season's harvest began to arrive in markets along with supplies from other parts of India, the death rate began a retreat, but it would remain high throughout 1944, boosted by famine's steadfast allies: cholera, smallpox, and malaria. Officially the tear in the natural fabric of Mother India lasted through 1946, well after the 721st said goodbye to their drawn lot in the war.

As Indian famines go, the Panchasher Manvantar may have been the worst since 1770, but it was a modest addition to the estimated total deaths from starvation under British rule.[10] From 1891 to 1941 twenty-five major famines claimed between thirty and forty million Indians in Tamil Nadu to the south, Bihar to the north, and Bengal to the east.[11]

. . .

The curious young men on the train, naïve know-it-alls and well-meaning quiet types, absorbed a nonstop depiction of anguish through their rolling portholes. Life in the mountains and countryside was hard, and people there were poor beyond American calculation. The animals were scrawny and the crops meager, but the real desperation played out in the cities and especially the railway stations.

People came to the stations to flee danger, to travel toward danger, and simply to have a roof over their heads. They carried their irreplaceable belongings in tattered blankets rolled for portage with the care of a lifetime. The abject poor, the beggars, the orphans, the sick, and the lame cried, "Baksheesh, baksheesh!" This anthem of desperation called forth in the minds of the soldiers a survival response of their own requirement. They reacted with emotional separation, objectification. This was war. Establishing emotional distance from the suffering around them was an involuntary defense, a sort of psychological shock absorber, a mechanism to save their American minds from a jolting derailment.

On the third day they pulled into Calcutta's railway station, Howrah. They detrained for a few hours while the engine tenders received water and coal. It was just long enough to confirm all their disappointment in India. Calcutta was as dirty and poor as Bombay, with the added confusion of wayward refugees. Chinese, Burmese, Indians, and British scurried through the pulsing terminal, parting the throng of beggars, the infirm, and the lame. The Americans were ready to leave long before their engines were.

4

To Parbatipur

Two feet, three inches: that was the only reason for Parbatipur to exist. This distance was the difference between the rails of metre-gauge line, mostly used by the tea planters of Assam, and the broad-gauge line running north from Calcutta, which was part of the backbone of India's national commerce. Here, amid the mud and bamboo huts, rice paddies and water buffalo, thousands of tons of freight were transshipped from one gauge to another, one boxcar or flatcar, tanker or hopper at a time, mostly using manual labor.

It was no way to run a railroad. But on this, the day of their arrival, the men of the 721st were less concerned with railroading and more concerned with food, water, shelter, and warmth.

When their train pulled into Parbatipur station on January 18, 1944, about a mile from the railroad yards, they took a siding. The order was passed, and 673 antsy, swivel-necked inmates escaped from the passenger coaches that had been their rolling pokey for five days. Before them stood twenty-seven forty-foot-square *bashas* (British campaign tents) surrounded by rice paddies. This two-acre parish of grass, canvas, wood, and earth surrounded by peasants and native laborers was to be their new quarters. The bashas were a modest proposition as construction goes but solidly middle class by Indian standards. The walls were made of interwoven bamboo strips and the roofs of thatched palm or grass tied to bamboo mats. The floors were dirt. Loose lattice protected open windows from large birds and playful monkeys who took great pleasure in scampering on the roof. Woven shutters were hung at the top of each window and could be propped open with three-foot sections of bamboo cane. Draped canvas covered the doorways. The beds were made of coconut-fiber rope strung over wooden frames with mosquito-net canopies. Each basha was partitioned into cramped, five-man cubicles.

The men quickly found their assigned quarters and began moving in, arranging their barracks bags, gas masks, carbines, and helmets to conserve space. They dug dog-eared family photographs out of their belongings and pinned them to the mat walls. Some hung rosaries and crosses and others glossy publicity shots of Hollywood starlets.

After eating their first meal from a hastily knocked-together field kitchen, the men wrapped themselves in thin wool blankets, curled into balls, and shivered the night away. The cool humidity of the Bengal air chilled their weary bones and kept at bay the good night's sleep they had all hoped to get. When morning arrived, it was not a fresh start.

The British had yet to finish the camp when the 721st arrived. There were no mess quarters, administrative buildings, proper showers, or latrines, so the men spent the first couple of weeks in work details finishing the camp to a bare minimum standard. Showers were a priority project. The motivated GIs soon had wells piped and pumps elevated. Empty five-gallon dehydrated-food containers with holes punched through their bottoms were hung overhead from wooden poles. Slatted wood flooring was laid over the packed earth as a touch of luxury, and pumping power was provided by any native within earshot for the price of a cigarette or an *anna*.[1] Given a few months, clever soldiers would rig a hot water system from a discarded locomotive boiler.

In a few days, as projects were completed and the camp made ready, the men found themselves with a bit of free time. They used this opportunity to build tables, clothing lockers, and stools.

Mail clerks from Headquarters and Service Company made daily trips to Calcutta, and in the evening men read or wrote letters in the bashas by the dim light of kerosene lamps and sat around small yellow campfires talking of the things soldiers will.

5

Air Raid

The blast was shrill and penetrating and came from high above the railroad station. It was the first time the soldiers had heard such a warning—their first air raid.

They dropped their evening meals where they squatted and laid down their pens on unfinished letters home. They kicked dirt on campfires and poured gallons of fresh coffee over coal fires used for heating water. They doused cooking stoves, cigarettes, and kerosene lanterns, anything marking them as targets for sharp-eyed Japanese air crew.

They ran in every direction all at once, grabbing their helmets and weapons and diving for cover. The guys in the motor pool raced engines and slipped clutches as they dispersed trucks and Jeeps to safe areas away from camp. Then they waited for the sound of approaching aircraft.

They never heard it, at least not that night.

As they waited in anticipation, the men focused on their training and emergency planning. Some prayed. Everyone tried to stay calm and do his job, and for the most part that's how it went. Some ended up in the wrong slit trenches, and some were caught without their helmets and arms, but the battalion assumed a sturdy defensive posture in a reasonable time.

The men of the 721st were not under attack, at least not by the Japanese Air Force. They had simply been exposed to a bit of unexpected and unanticipated Indian railroad culture. The whistle that had set them in frantic motion was a signal of sorts, but not for an air raid. It was a call for the Bengal and Assam wreck crew to assemble because somewhere along the line there had been an accident. Other than the spilled coffee and rattled nerves, for the 721st it was a cheap lesson and a good drill.

6

The Ledo Road

The setting was humble; the mission was anything but. The construction of a logistical lifeline from India to China known as the Ledo Road was at the heart of "the greatest engineering undertaking of the War."

Construction had begun on October 29, 1942, fifteen months before the arrival of the 721st, on the orders of Gen. Joseph Stilwell, the commander of U.S. forces in the China-Burma-India theater. The idea was to build a road over which the Allies could support the Chinese national forces under the command of Generalissimo Chiang Kai-shek. The idea came from Chiang, who estimated building the road would take five months.[1]

In December 1942 the Joint Chiefs of Staff ordered men and equipment for the Ledo Road project, which they ranked second in priority right behind Eisenhower's North African campaign.[2] The army estimated that Stilwell would need 6,000 construction troops to get the job done and rushed them to the CBI. Stilwell turned the Ledo Road project over to his logistics specialist, Lt. Gen. Raymond Wheeler, who had been his student at West Point, where Stilwell had taught Chinese in the Language Department. The two men got along well, and Wheeler had earned a good reputation as a road builder for his work in the Argonne Forest during World War I.[3]

When work began in mid-December 1942 Wheeler used the 823rd Engineer Aviation Battalion to clear the road trace. This battalion was followed by the Forty-fifth Regiment, which completed the grading and applied metaling stone, a mix of natural gravel and crushed rock, to stabilize the road's surface. Both construction outfits were made up of African American soldiers with white officers.[4] Wheeler established Base Section 3 at Ledo and placed Brig. Gen. John Arrowsmith in charge.[5]

The road trace reached the Burma-India border at mile 43.2 from Ledo on February 28, 1943. Col. Ferdinand Tate fired his pistol into the air to mark the crossing into Japanese-held territory, and as the lead D-4 bulldozer chugged into Burma a bugler from the 823rd sounded "To the Colors." Alongside the roadway enlisted men hammered a sign to a banyan tree that read, "Welcome to Burma. This Way to Tokyo."[6]

The 823rd and Forty-fifth were joined by the Chinese Tenth Independent Combat Engineer Regiment in March. The Chinese unit arrived without equipment and was put to work with hand tools clearing trace. The rains came early in 1943, and by the first week of April the monsoon was fully upon them. Construction work became all but impossible. From the end of March to mid-August 1943 the construction road head—that muddy point where men and bulldozers were attacking the forest and mountains—had progressed from mile 47.3 to mile 50.7, less than four miles.[7]

The road builders faced all of the hardships of a battlefield plus malaria, dysentery, and construction accidents.[8] Their world was monotonous yet unpredictable. The rain, mud, heat, humidity, and mildew were constant unwelcome companions. They were isolated in a strange country and way out of their element, unenthusiastic visitors in a land previously known only to curious headhunters, hungry wildlife, and Japanese patrols.

In October 1943 Stilwell shook things up, replacing General Arrowsmith with Col. Lewis A. Pick, an aggressive road builder who knew a lot about drainage. Pick moved his command post to the road head and reinstated around-the-clock operations. He told his troops that "rain, mud and malaria be damned, the road was going to be built," and he implemented innovative construction and procurement techniques. He and his men finished the job five days ahead of schedule. On December 27, 1943, the road reached Shingbwiyang, 103 miles from Ledo. The first convoy brought candy, doughnuts, and 9,600 cans of beer.[9] But they were still more than 1,000 miles from Chongqing.

By the time the 721st was organizing its camp, the construction of the Ledo Road, although a long way from finished, was back on track and promising to complete the lifeline to China. The job of the 721st was to provide the matériel to send down the road.

7

Relay

The 721st Railway Operating Battalion was like the first runner in a great relay race to defeat the Japanese. They took the hand-off from Calcutta at Parbatipur; there they transshipped all the freight from broad-gauge to metre-gauge equipment, then ran the freight baton 120 miles down the track, passed it off to the 725th, who ran it 175 miles and handed off to the 726th, who ran it 160 miles to the 745th, who covered 108 miles for their lap and delivered it to the 748th for the final 100-mile leg of the race to Ledo.

From Ledo freight would travel by truck—once the road was finished—or over the hump by air transport. Either way, freight was the lifeblood of the Allies' war effort. If it stopped, so did the heart of the combat units—American, Chinese, British, and Indian—that depended upon it. Without the ability to supply fighting units, all was lost—as the Japanese would discover in the approaching months.

So how did American railroaders get the assignment of running an Indian railroad? After all, the Indians had been railroading for nearly as long as the Americans and surely knew the local situation much better than solidly educated, working-class guys from scrubbed-clean America. How was it that the prosecution of the war in CBI depended upon Americans running the Bengal and Assam Railroad?

The answer to that question had begun to take shape five months earlier, in August 1943, when the Allies met in Quebec at a conference code-named Quadrant. The biggest news out of Quadrant was the decision to go forward with a cross-Channel attack to retake Europe codenamed Overlord. The next biggest news was that British vice admiral Lord Louis Mountbatten was named supreme commander of the Allied forces in Southeast Asia, in

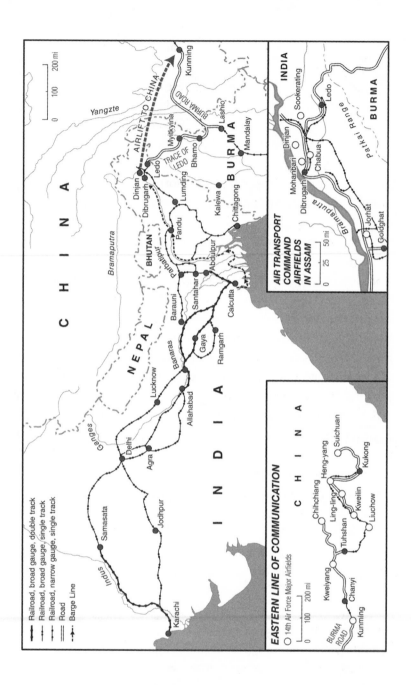

MAP 3. Allied lines of communication in the China-Burma-India theater.
Map by Erin Greb.

charge of all British, Chinese, Indian, and U.S. forces in the China-Burma-India theater.

The grand plan to defeat the Japanese remained the same: retake China, bomb the Japanese home islands, then invade from Korea. But the British and Americans had different approaches. The Americans wanted to take northern Burma, then advance on Rangoon, thus opening a quick resupply route to China. The British wanted the Americans and Chinese to take northern Burma, then bypass Rangoon and take Singapore. They weren't interested in a dreary slog through the swamps of southern Burma.[1]

The issue was presented to the Allied Combined Chiefs of Staff (CCS), who wanted a line of communication that would support air operations in China and ground operations in Burma. At the same time they wanted to build a communications system across northern Burma. These plans depended on construction of the Ledo Road, as they stated in their staff study: "The opening of an overland route to China will greatly facilitate operations and may well assist in bringing hostilities to an earlier conclusion than would otherwise be possible."[2]

The Americans at General Somervell's Service of Supply told the CCS they had no doubt that the Assam line of communications could be quickly improved. They called the target figure of 3,400 tons per day by November 1, 1943, "insignificant." The British thought it nearly impossible.[3]

The CCS accepted Somervell's ambitious projections and ordered an increase in the Assam line of communications to 220,000 tons a month by January 1, 1946. To accomplish this ambitious mission it was decided that Americans should be in charge and provide the men and matériel to make it happen. After the Quadrant Conference Somervell began negotiating with the British and Indians about who would be in charge of what in order to get the supplies through. When he first proposed taking over sections of the Bengal and Assam line, the Indian government vetoed the plan. When the British sided with the Indians, Somervell found negotiations at an impasse.[4]

But the freight had to get through. In October 1943 Somervell met with Lord Mountbatten and pointed out that a 50 percent increase in tonnage would be required by April 1944 if the Allies were to keep their commitments to China. Mountbatten asked if British and Indian railway officials could guarantee such an increase. They demurred. With no other options, Mountbatten ordered that U.S. troops take over the operation of the railroad. A Military Railway Service was established for the Bengal and Assam line between Katihar and Ledo. Other specialized units were ordered that would build a petroleum pipeline, operate barges where the railroad crossed rivers, and handle the port operations in Calcutta. It was ordered that U.S. units would begin operating the railroad on March 1, 1944.[5]

The Bengal and Assam Railway was owned by the state except for a thirty-mile section at the end of the line, between Tinsukia and Ledo, which was in private hands. Prior to the war it mainly serviced the tea plantations in Assam and typically carried perhaps three trains a day. Broad-gauge double track ran northward from the shipping port of Calcutta to Abdulpur, where it became single track and continued to Parbatipur. There the line turned eastward and became metre-gauge all the way to Ledo. At Parbatipur all freight was transshipped from broad-gauge to metre-gauge equipment as the rolling stock was incompatible on the two differently gauged tracks.

From Parbatipur the railroad's single-track main line paralleled the mighty Brahmaputra River for nearly 600 miles, crossing to the south bank at Pandu by ferry. There was another crossing of a tributary river just west of Ledo. From Parbatipur the line also ventured south to Akhaura, then northeast, finally reconnecting to the main line at Lumding. It was from this southerly loop that the British forces at Imphal received their supplies.

The Bengal and Assam Railway comprised a total trackage of 3,478 miles. Of this, the 738 miles from Calcutta to Ledo would be the military backbone. The section from Parbatipur to Ledo and all the connecting branch lines, a total of 804 miles, would be operated by the U.S. Army's Military Railway Service.[6] They would join two other MRSs already operating, one in the European theater, the other in Iran.

So the plan was set and the politics settled. The U.S. Army would be in charge of moving the weight of war over foreign fields and streams in a land as unlike America as any had seen.

The Japanese had their own plans and a pretty good idea of what the Allies were up to. Stilwell had been training his ill-equipped Chinese troops in Chongqing for nearly seventeen months and nearly as long in Ledo. On the Allies' side, many thought an offensive was long overdue. Following Quadrant, Gen. George C. Marshall, U.S. Army chief of staff, told Stilwell to prepare to occupy northern Burma. D-Day for the operation would be mid-February 1944.[7]

Marshall wanted overland communications with China via the occupation of the city of Myitkyina. He put the job of recapturing northern Burma in General Stilwell's hands. Providing the supplies to get the job done would be in the hands of the 721st and America's soldier railroaders.

8

First Encounters

First encounters between the brash Americans and the proud Indians were not always easy. Jim Hantzis had to muster all the politeness and polish he had when he introduced himself and his squad from Company B to the foreman of the Bengal and Assam locomotive shop. The tall, dark-skinned, turbaned Indian looked to Hantzis to be around forty years old. His face was deeply scarred from the corner of his left eye down his sunken cheek. Hantzis was pretty sure it was from a knife wound, probably from a dagger like the one the man had tucked into his waist sash. The Indian was unmoved, uncommunicative, and generally unfriendly.

After introducing himself, Hantzis asked the foreman, "And what is your name, sir?"

The stone-faced man returned a cold stare.

"With your permission, my men and I would like to watch the work being done here and in the locomotive repair shop, sir."

The foreman twitched his handlebar mustache while holding Hantzis with his unflinching stare. Hantzis took the mustache twitch to be as close to a *yes* as he was going to get and slowly turned to face his men. With the tall Indian towering behind him, arms folded, he told the men, "Okay, fan out and find your work areas. Stay out of the way and let the locals do their jobs. Do not interfere. Do not argue. Just observe and take some notes on how we can"—he paused to find the right words, aware that the looming foreman spoke excellent English when he wished—"help out. Meet back at the mess tent at twelve hundred hours. And don't start any trouble. Just smile and stay out of the way."

And with those instructions, Hantzis turned to face the foreman, smiled, and nodded his head. The foreman stared down his long nose at the young American, turned his back, and walked away.

Hantzis slowly turned back to face the men. A lanky private off the Atchison–Topeka & Santa Fe in Kansas City, George Lee, removed his cap, scratched the top of his head, and said in a dry, rural monotone, "Well, that fellow was sure friendly, Sarge."

In the back of the group a young machinist off the Baltimore & Ohio in Cumberland, Maryland, Alvin Carder, snickered, "He's big stuff today, but we'll see how important he thinks he is come March 1." Then, sweeping his arm in a grand motion before him, Carder exclaimed, "Look at these guys. They're just standing around. There ain't a bit of work getting done here. They must have a hell of a union, Sarge."

Hantzis looked at Carder, then at Lee, shook his head ever so slightly and raised his left eyebrow. As first encounters go, it had been pretty standard railroad stuff.

9

Inside the 721st

The 721st Railway Operating Battalion was composed of four companies. Company A worked on trackage, with two platoons for right of way and one for bridges. Company B worked in the shop crafts, repairing and outfitting locomotives, rolling stock, and other railroad equipment. They were machinists, boilermakers, blacksmiths, electricians, car knockers, and helpers. Two of their three platoons worked on engines and tenders, and the other shopped rolling stock. Company C contained the operating crafts and was the largest company in the battalion, made up of engineers, brakemen, conductors, and firemen. Headquarters and Service Company (H&S) worked office duty and logistical support and included block station operators, telegraphers, and dispatchers.[1] As they got to work they saw many challenges awaiting them.

When the battalion had left Bombay, the men in Company A's three platoons noted the difference between American and Indian techniques used to build tracks: the placement of joints. Joints are the connecting steel bars that tie sections of rails together. They make the reassuring *clickety-clack* on a well-run railroad, but they can also make big problems. In America rail joints are staggered, but in India, they are placed directly across from each other, allowing the track to sink into washouts much more easily, making for all kinds of maintenance headaches, rough rides, and derailments.

The men of Company B spent the month of February getting familiar with the Indian system. They assessed the types of equipment, maintenance routines, and shop and machine tools. What few tools the Americans had on hand, mostly hammers, wrenches, and other odd bits, were borrowed from the battalion's small supply. Without their tools, even had they wanted to help out, they weren't going to do anything but get in the way.

The hodgepodge of locomotives used by the Indians came from manufacturers in England, Germany, Belgium, France, and Czechoslovakia. The rolling stock was equally diverse. Most of the equipment was new to the Americans, so the inquisitive mechanical minds of Company B were well stimulated.

The engine and train crews of Company C learned the traffic control block system, Indian signals, and the layout of the railroad. Traffic control on the Bengal and Assam Railway was unique, thanks to Alan Neale, an inventive engineer who had worked on the Great Indian Peninsular Railroad long ago. Neale's contribution to the safe movement of trains was nearly foolproof, a considerable accomplishment given the literacy level of the typical Indian stationmaster. The ingenious Neale Ball Token System would require the operating crafts of the 721st, who thought of themselves as old dogs in the automated, high-tech U.S. traffic control, to learn new tricks.

H&S Company prepared to station their trainmasters, telegraphers, dispatchers, and clerks. Along with supervising the operation of the railroad, they had to work out a system to provision the battalion and keep the paperwork flowing up the chain of command.

. . .

The Indian system had many areas where the need for improvement was obvious, to American eyes at any rate. For example, floodlighting was installed in the transshipment yards in preparation for around-the-clock operations.[2] But one of the craziest things about Indian railroaders, something that drove the enlisted Americans up the wall, was their lack of work ethic and their disregard for timetables. This lack of discipline and urgency would bewilder the hard-charging GIs for months to come. But while the 721st bided their time as patiently as possible and suffered through a campwide epidemic of dysentery, there was one timetable that would not be ignored: the war.

10

Merrill's Marauders

In the predawn darkness recon squads fanned out to scout the point and parallel the flanks. The commanding officer of First Battalion, Lt. Col. William Osborne, gave them time to get into position, then gave the order to move out.

The remainder of the Intelligence and Reconnaissance Platoon formed the head of the column. With this order they took the first steps of a forty-mile march across Japanese-held northern Burma to a tiny village called Tanja Ga. Before their return in August they would cover more than 700 miles.

The First Battalion was made up of volunteers from the States and, just like the two battalions that would follow, was organized into two combat teams. The remainder of I&R preceded a rifle platoon, followed by a rifle company with half the heavy weapons platoon. The combat team headquarters and medical detachments filled in the middle of the snaking line. These vulnerable units were followed by another rifle platoon and the remainder of the heavy weapons troops.

At 0900 hours Second Battalion, volunteers from Panama and Trinidad, repeated the jump-off, followed by Third Battalion, made up of combat veterans, at 1100 hours. Each battalion brought 35 officers, 928 enlisted men, 139 horses or mules, 181 carbines, 7 heavy machine guns, 6 light machine guns, 102 submachine guns, 10 60mm mortars, 7 81mm mortars, 4 pistols, 54 Browning Automatic Rifles, 624 M-1 rifles, and 6 rockets.[1]

The highly trained special troops of this unique regiment would go against battle-tested veteran soldiers of General Mutaguchi's entrenched Eighteenth Division. They would fight five major battles and thirty minor engagements from February to August 1944 and win every time.

They lived and died under the constant threat of jungle ambush. They carried their sick and wounded for days until they reached clearings and sandbars where flimsy light aircraft could land and evacuate the worst cases. They climbed over mountains as high as 7,000 feet, hacking pathways as they went, and attacked without rest at the end of the trail. They kept moving even while their uniforms, boots, and packs rotted from the heat and damp. They kept moving even while their flesh did the same.

Collectively these volunteers were known as the 5307th Composite Unit (Provisional) of the Army of the United States, code-named Galahad, under the command of Frank Merrill. Clever journalists and an admiring public quickly came to know them as Merrill's Marauders.

It is not surprising that the Marauders were an American version of Orde Wingate's Chindits, for that eccentric, hard-as-nails Britisher supervised the overall preparation of the unit. The Marauders were the first U.S. special operations troops and the only U.S. ground combat troops in CBI in February 1944. Just like the Chindits, the Marauders were a long-range penetration unit whose supply line would be by hook or crook and mostly by air. Their supplies would arrive in Ledo by rail, then be flown to radio-designated drop points by brave air crew in overburdened, unarmored, slow-moving transports.

Recruiting for the 5307th began in September 1943, when General Marshall on behalf of the president of the United States called for volunteers "of a high state of physical ruggedness and stamina" to undertake a "hazardous mission" and promised that every volunteer would be promoted a grade in rank.[2] Nine hundred fifty veterans of Guadalcanal and New Guinea signed up for the unit, and a similar number came from service on Trinidad and Puerto Rico with the Caribbean Defense Command. Roughly the same number volunteered from highly trained units of the Army Ground Forces in the United States.

The Marauders arrived in Bombay on October 31, 1943, then moved about 125 miles inland to Deolali to begin training. Their initial regimen focused on physical conditioning and close-order drills; by December they were tough enough to jump into the fight. In final preparations for jungle operations they moved on to central India and the village of Deogarh in Madhya Pradesh. There they spent ten days with Wingate and his Chindits. Their maneuvers in Deogarh were designed to uncover shortcomings, and Wingate, the ultimate provocateur, was a master at unmasking weaknesses. Deficiencies in the untested force were promptly addressed, and changes were made in communications and command. Most important, the men got their first taste of what maneuvering and fighting would be like in what many considered the most inhospitable terrain of World War II.

Training was physically demanding. Calisthenics and marches with full packs were par for the course. Every soldier drilled on marksmanship, scouting, map reading, jungle navigation, stream crossing, demolition, concealment, and camouflage. Then they cross-trained so that rifle platoon leaders could direct mortar fire, demolitions specialists could operate radios, and everybody could fill in when the going got rough, which it did in short order. They trained for small unit attacks against entrenched enemy positions. The Marauders would see combat that was swift and at quarters so close you could smell the enemy. Leadership had to be aggressive, and squads and platoons had to be cohesive and confident. Many units had to be reorganized and soldiers reassigned to break up cliques formed in the units from which they had volunteered.

Just like all things CBI, the formation of the 5307th was not without its politics and controversy. America needed combat troops in the theater to satisfy pressure from the British and Chinese who, until February 1944, had been doing all the fighting. At the Quadrant Conference in Quebec it was decided that the Americans would put together a combat regiment code-named Galahad and place it under Wingate's command. That, of course, infuriated Stilwell, who didn't particularly like Wingate's exhibitionist style or his planned use of the unit. Wingate saw the 5307th as an isolated attack force, but Stilwell wanted to use it in conjunction with his main force of Chinese, as a flanking force or a spearhead.

It wasn't until early January that command authority was firmly in Stilwell's hands, and on January 6, 1944, the general ruffled some feathers in his own ranks by removing Col. Charles N. Hunter from command and assigning his operations officer, Brig. Gen. Frank Merrill, to take charge.[3] Soon thereafter Stilwell ordered the 5307th to close in on Ledo by February 7, and from there to march down the Ledo Road as far as Ningbyen.

The unit left the training area at Deogarh almost immediately on the heels of Stilwell's directive. With their departure they left behind thick forests, the Vindhya and Satpura hills, and terrain so inaccessible and remote that it was home to the most primitive, Stone Age aboriginal Indian tribes to be found anywhere. In this it was a perfect prelude to the eight months to come.

Their 1,000-mile trip was by train, barge, and foot and took almost a month. They passed through Parbatipur as the 721st was setting up and getting ready to railroad. In a few months the Marauders' return to Deogarh along the same railroad, only this time with Yanks in charge, would be an especially memorable and, to some, shocking event. Even on their way to Ledo the Marauders gave a glimpse of their rebellious underpinnings. The unit, after all, had a reputation for being an aggregate of misfits and troublemakers, a perception reinforced when some in their ranks took potshots at Indians from the windows of their rail cars.[4]

Stilwell's first mission for the 5307th was to support the Twenty-second and Thirty-eighth Chinese divisions pushing the Japanese southward out of northern Burma. The Marauders were to march forty miles eastward along jungle and valley trails, turn south and then back west to encircle the Japanese. Stilwell wanted them to establish roadblocks on the Kamaing Road somewhere near Walawbum, thus cutting off any Japanese retreat and resupply.

The Marauders made it to Tanja Ga, a village about one-third of the way to Walawbum, on the afternoon of February 28. There they received orders from Stilwell to get to Walawbum as quickly as possible; the Chinese were making better progress than expected, and Stilwell needed the Marauders to get into position quickly so he could take full advantage of the Japanese retreat. The Marauders immediately shoved off for Tanja Ga without a moment's rest.

In Stilwell's world timetables were not subject to auspiciousness or philosophical interpretation. They were best adhered to if not exceeded. A stern disposition, a demand for accountability, and an unyielding temperament may have made it difficult for Vinegar Joe to win friends and influence others, but it was a fine fit and a welcome proposition to America's soldier railroaders.

11

Company B

The men of Company B took their mission seriously. While the other companies of the 721st chipped away at inefficiencies in paperwork, operations, and construction, Company B made sure that everything rolled faster, better, smoother, and longer than anything the Bengal and Assam Railway had ever seen before. Their first priority was motive power. Steam locomotives make the power to move their driver pistons, apply brakes, sound the whistle, and steep Darjeeling tea for an appreciative crew by boiling water. The system works like this.

Something combustible (usually coal but sometimes wood) goes into the firebox below a boiler and heats the water to boiling; power-wise, you then have something to work with. It's a tidy system and not all that complicated. The system depends on efficiently boiling the water and containing the steam until it is needed for power.

But boiling water causes problems. In the real world, besides H_2O, water is full of minerals, sediments, metals, and bothersome impurities that stay around after the water has boiled away as steam. In India water was often no more than high-grade mud, which created problems until the GIs drilled deep wells to improve its purity. Still, gunk has to end up somewhere, and it could usually be found fouling the walls and floor of a boiler. Fouling is prevented by *washouts*.

Fouling decreases a locomotive's efficiency, which means the engine burns more coal to pull the freight. Fouling, and its accompanying foam, can also cause an engineer to misread his locomotive's water level and incorrectly inject cold water into the boiler. The operational temperature of a submerged crown sheet—the heavy piece of metal that is the top of the firebox and the bottom of the boiler—is in the neighborhood of 600 degrees Fahrenheit. But without water in the boiler to dissipate the heat, the temperature of the metal rises to that of the fire below: 2,200 degrees. Injecting cold water at this temperature can make a boiler explode.

A clean boiler is also a fuel-efficient boiler. In India in 1944 coal was not an easy commodity to come by. In fact before the Americans took over, the Bengal and Assam engine crews were paid bonuses for not using coal. So a pay-conscious Indian engineer would fire a boiler to build a head of steam, run the engine until it stopped, then fire another boiler so as not to overuse the fuel. Cost-effective? Hard to say. But it was definitely not the way to run a railroad.

In 1939 India mined about one million tons of coal. Most of it came from deep shaft mines up to 150 miles inland from Calcutta. The coal moved by rail to Calcutta and was there loaded onto ships that plied the eastern and western coastal waterways of the subcontinent, delivering the fuel. With the coming of the war this valuable cargo was too vulnerable to move over open water, so it was instead transported by rail.[1] But the railroads weren't up to the task. So coal was a scarce commodity, and its efficient use was critical.

Some of the locomotives the 721st inherited from the Bengal and Assam operation were victims of shoddy repairs and stingy maintenance and were on the verge of needing a boiler heart transplant when Company B took over the shop. With their newly arrived tools in hand, the GIs instituted a bimonthly washout schedule. This precaution was doubly necessary because of the coal shortage and the dirty water of northeastern India.

A typical washout takes the better part of a day and requires the removal of a series of plugs in the boiler's walls, into which a stream of high-pressure cleaning solution is sprayed. It's labor-intensive work, but it's the smart thing to do if you want the trains to run dependably. Company B performed mechanical triage on the tired old fleet to save what they could.

Because a locomotive, no matter how well maintained, can't pull without coal, the men began hoarding the black gold. Soon they had a stockpile of the scarce commodity, around which armed guards patrolled twenty-four hours a day to keep away locals who coveted the fuel. Other railroad items were also at risk for theft, for example, the journal box. A journal box is the part of a railroad car where the wheel axle rides in its bushings or friction bearings. As the axle turns, bearing the weight of the car, it generates friction that is eased by filling the box with a heavy lubricant. If the lubricant, called "dope," goes missing because of leaks, mistakes, or whatever, the axle's bushing—the machined bearing the axle rides on—will heat to the point that it glows red and eventually ignites the remaining dope or sets something next to the journal box on fire.

In India it was necessary to rivet or bolt journal box covers closed because the locals would steal the dope to build fires and fuel cooking stoves. Journal box covers in the United States were a flip-up design, and filling the bearing reservoir with dope took very little time. But in India Company B had to work around the security problem and found that cutting the bolts or rivets with an acetylene torch made this routine maintenance a tad quicker, saving forty-five minutes on each four-journal car using this method.

Company B also designed special guard cages and welded them over the locomotives' headlights to prevent locals from stealing the bulbs. What they did with the stolen bulbs is anybody's guess. While working at the front of the locomotive, the conscientious GIs—leery of fire—installed spark arrestors on the engine stacks. Inside the locomotives they installed lighting and protective guards around the boiler water glasses and gauges. On the locomotives issued by the U.S. War Department the men installed quick-release air valves that cut the bleed time from five minutes to thirty seconds. Prior to Pearl Harbor, these 2-8-2 Baldwin engines were affectionately known as Mikados or Mikes. For obvious reasons these trusty giants gained a new patriotic nickname, MacArthurs, literally overnight. They were damn good engines. Some are still in use on the Indian railway system and throughout Southeast Asia to this day.

Using Alemite fittings and air pressure made other types of

lubrication faster. Instead of hand-packing a bearing, Company B used air pressure to power a grease nozzle that connected to a one-way nipple coupler. The installation of the coupler required a fair amount of machining, but once installed it saved a lot of time. Air pressure forced lubricant into a joint via the U.S.-style fitting very quickly and provided positive displacement of the old lubricant. This modification reduced the time required for the job and provided far better protection. Compressed air was also used to the battalion's advantage when they refired cold boilers after washouts and other maintenance. Blowing air across the fuel and accelerating combustion quickly ignited the coal, which allowed the boiler to raise steam and power the locomotive in an hour and forty-five minutes instead of the usual five hours.

Many of the locomotives that had seen service on the Bengal and Assam, although they were in running order, were not efficient. Company B reworked these engines, aligning and machining connecting rods and valves to the higher U.S. standards. While this rework required a significant investment of time in the beginning, it saved time down the road by reducing additional maintenance and improving the efficiency and power of the reworked units. Because of Company B's *fix it right* approach, drop pit work fell by 80 percent.

Maintenance and repairs depend on a steady supply of parts and materials. Company B had difficulty getting timely deliveries from the repair supplies store at Saidpur, a small railroad town about nine miles to the north of Parbatipur and the home of a detachment of the 758th Shop Battalion. Supplies and repairs at Saidpur were often handled by Indian crews, and like much of the work done by the Indians throughout the railroad a lack of urgency and repeated delays drove the Americans nuts. So the 721st arranged their own deliveries and fashioned a Jeep to run on rails and tow a small wagon for part runs. They had to be careful with the handy little vehicle because once the rig got rolling the inadequate braking power of the lightweight Jeep made for a treacherous ride, especially on wet rails.

Company B set out to improve the rolling stock as soon as the

motive power had received its necessary attention. Basic maintenance was the order of the day, but one design deficiency quickly
drew the company's attention. The Americans reworked the odd
screw-and-link coupling devices used on the Indian wagons to
make the routine job of connecting cars together, a dangerous but
relatively quick operation with U.S. equipment, a little less labori-
ous and risky. But no matter how much Company B improved on
the existing Indian equipment, that equipment alone would never
allow them to meet the tonnage goals set by the chiefs of staff. It
was simply too old, too small, and too long out of date.

12

Fire

"Have you seen this crap?" S.Sgt. Nels Whittaker asked Jim Hantzis, closing the door of the shop battalion's office behind him. Brushing off the dust from the afternoon's festering storm, Whittaker continued without looking up, "A roundhouse wallah, one of my freight handlers, just brought me this and asked if we were going to leave him behind? The poor guy dropped to his knees and begged me not to leave! I had two other wallahs disappear on me last week, just high-tailed it without a word."

Hantzis gave Whittaker a puzzled look, put down the clipboard he held in his right hand, and took the ragged piece of yellowed paper. He examined both sides, then read the front.

C. 215

The Capture of the Assam Province is Near

The City of Imphal!

Imphal, the most important advance base of the Anglo-Indian Forces, was completely captured by the Indo-Nippon Units. What the Britishers called, The Impregnable 4th Army Corps was annihilated to the very last soldier. The Indo-Japanese Units without resting are again advancing toward Ledo, Dimapur, Silchar, Dacca from 5 different directions. The Assam railroad line will be intercepted within a few days. Then before the monsoon arrives, the capture of the Assam Province will be completely executed. You are now in the very verge of life or death since your life-line, retreating roads are now in our hands. You are now placed in such a position that you could never acquire nor hope for any help, food, or supply of arms from outside. In concert with the Indian National Army, the Indian Masses at various parts of

India are now revolting against the British. Numberless Indian soldiers are running from the British Army and are joining the Indian National Army. With sticks and stones, the Indian Masses without arms are killing the Britishers.

Again we proclaim. DEATH OR SURRENDER?

Nippon Army.[1]

Hantzis read the propaganda carefully, shaking his head all the while. Then he reached into the top drawer of the old wooden desk behind which he was seated, pulled out a piece of paper of similar quality, and handed it to his friend:

To You The English Soldiers!

You are like fishes caught in a net, without an outlet. The only faith left for you is Death alone. When we think and give consideration about your loving wives, parents and brothers we could never carry on inhuman-like actions. Therefore stop your useless resistance. Throw down your arms, and surrender. It is then that we will guarantee your lives and will treat you according to the International Law.

How to surrender to the Jpanese Forces

1. The surrenderers are required to come hoisting some white cloth or holding up both hands.

2. Carry the rifle on the shoulder upside down.

3. Show his bill to the Japanese soldier.

Nippon Army.[2]

Whittaker finished reading and handed the paper back. With a bitter smirk on his face and his thin mustache rising nearly to his right cheek, Whittaker said, "I hope the sorry son of a bitch who checked the spelling had the *honorable* chance to commit harakiri. He didn't even spell *Japanese* correctly. *That* ought to piss off Tojo!"

Hantzis chuckled, but in a concerned tone he confided, "I guess they lost a few more skittish wallahs in Company C. A track foreman told me that he barely had enough for a crew last week. And he said they caught a couple nonlocals carting off fuses and kerosene."

"Shit," said Whittaker. "With all the supplies coming through this place, I'm surprised half of it doesn't wind up on the black market in Calcutta."

"Yeah, but these guys were—" Hantzis stopped, not wanting to spread unsettling rumors.

"I know what you mean," Whittaker assured him. "I talked to that foreman too, the tall guy from Ohio, right?"

Hantzis nodded.

"He said there was something about those guys that made him very nervous," Whittaker went on. "The foreman didn't think they were your garden-variety thieves or poachers. Both of them were packing those crappy Nip Nambu Luger knockoffs. The MPs had 'em locked up for a couple days here in the brig, and rumor has it they shipped 'em up to Stilwell at Ledo, you know."

Hantzis wondered aloud, "Two down, how many to go?" He leaned back in his desk chair, laced his fingers behind his head, and started to lift his feet up to the pull-out wing of his desk when the wooden door of the Company B building was flung open, slamming against the outer frame and startling both men inside.

A small dust devil swept into the office as a young private from H&S Company stuck his head inside and yelled, "The camp's on fire!" then leaped from the three-step entrance riser, leaving the door open, and raced to the next building.

Hantzis and Whittaker looked at each other for a split second, stunned, then rushed to the doorway. The dust storm had grown more intense since Whittaker's arrival, and the wind now blew the tiny particles of earth with the force of a sandblaster. Peering toward the camp about a half-mile away, they could barely make out a gray plume rising above the treetops. Whittaker muttered, "Shhhit!"

The two men almost knocked each other down getting through the door. As they raced toward the camp the smell of burning bamboo, canvas, and kerosene grew stronger. Halfway there Hantzis began to think about what he wanted to save, if he could, from his basha. The only thing he could think of was the ivory bracelet he had bought for Marilou from an old Sikh in Bombay and her photo tied to a tent pole.

The camp was made of highly combustible materials—bamboo, wood, and canvas—and all of it was like tinder. The weather had been very dry. The wind from that afternoon's dust storm was gusting to more than fifty miles per hour. The flames swept across the camp with the speed of frenetic demons, engulfing the camp so quickly it looked like one giant bonfire as the men approached. Through the blinding dust and smoke they could see that the fire was most fierce near the mess hall on the western perimeter.

About half of the battalion had arrived before Hantzis and Whittaker. Some men were trying in vain to swat out the flames with shirts and jackets, but their waving was only adding to the commotion. Bucket lines had started forming, but the fire equipment had yet to arrive.

In the midst of certain calamity Hantzis was granted a small stroke of luck. Since Company B had been the last to join the camp they were housed in the newest construction, on the eastern perimeter. The fire had begun on the western edge of camp, and a few bashas on the eastern side along with the Battalion Headquarters and officer housing were still untouched. They would be the last consumed.

A corner of the western wall of Hantzis's basha had just started to burn. Whittaker, whose cot and locker were opposite the flames, knew what his friend was thinking and tried to stop him. He grabbed his arm and yelled, "Greek, don't go in there, you'll get trapped."

But Hantzis knew what he was after.

As he entered the smoky basha he took a deep breath and held it. He could barely see because the smoke stung his eyes. Amid the crackling of the flames he could hear dozens of rounds of small arms' ammunition exploding throughout the camp. He found his footlocker, dug deep into the gear and clothing packed inside, and felt the pouch with the bracelet. He withdrew his hand clutching the pouch and as a second thought grabbed his camera. Then he grabbed the photograph of Marilou, folded it in half top to bottom, and ripped it away from the pole, tearing it in two.

Hunkered over, crouched in a duck walk, he made it to the tent's entranceway just as its rolled-up overhead canvas cover burst into flames. It fell to the wooden steps just behind his last footfall with a pernicious thud. He ran twenty yards or so, gasping for air all the way, back to where Whittaker and two other sergeants were standing and dropped to his hands and knees, coughing.

When he finally stopped coughing, Hantzis looked sideways back at the fire and saw a few men racing into untouched bashas attempting to retrieve personal treasures. Soon the entire colony of twenty-seven bashas was in flames. Only two that were set apart from the main camp by a wide roadway remained untouched.

The fire raged for thirty minutes before the men gained control. No sooner had the flames run their course than it started to rain, the first rain in days. Before long it became a drenching rain of biblical intensity that soon turned the camp's ground into ankle-deep mud and made recovery of the few salvageable items left behind even more difficult. Undeterred, the men rummaged through the smoldering remains, hoping to find anything of value, anything they could still use.

In the ashes of the Subsistence Warehouse they recovered charred containers of K and C Rations. Their contents, food that even under normal conditions was far from appetizing, was baked and hardened, but it was all that was to be had for that night's chow.

Later that evening, a carload of supplies arrived from the 725th Railroad Operating Battalion at Lalmanirhat. It was a godsend.

The camp's commander of the guard, a Sergeant Allen, posted sentries to ward off Indian looters. Captain Kerr of C Company rounded up his men and moved them to an area two miles west of Parbatipur to share accommodations with the pipeliners of the 776th Engineer Petroleum Distribution Company. Part of Company B crowded into two of the undamaged bashas for the night, and the remainder went to sleep in the locomotive and car repair sheds. H&S Company made due with just one basha. The remaining officers and enlisted men slept in railroad cars in Parbatipur Yard.[3]

As dawn arrived, the rays of daylight revealed the sublime devastation. The camp had been leveled, and the ground on which it stood was charred like a briquette. It was as if Angi, the Hindu god of fire, had demanded a sacrifice of the outsiders—invaders of his kingdom—then erased the soldiers' worldly possessions from the face of the earth.

With the coming of the new day inventory parties were organized and additional tents were erected to house B and H&S Companies. Company B's Orderly Room became the Battalion Headquarters. The men from H&S Company built furniture and set up an office in an undamaged basha on the southwest corner of the camp. Their new quarters would eventually become Battalion Headquarters, Post Exchange, and Company Supply.

The men of the 721st shook off their initial shock, quickly pulled together, and got to work. But the salvage and rebuilding operation would take more than five months, and the tedious process of reconstructing battalion records and finally improving the camp would take much longer. Yet through all the confusion and hardship the railroad never stopped running. Not a train was canceled. Night and day, day and night, the railroad ran.

Hantzis wrote to Marilou a year after the fire:

> The excitement of the fire had died down and it was raining off and on. The fellows were taking stock of what they managed to save out of the fire and were improvising places to spend the night. Out of four of us, me, Hammond, Nelson and Ferree, we managed to save enough to rig up a shelter half, a pup tent to you. Hammond and Nels each saved half of their shelter halves and me and Ferree saved our blankets and mosquito net, so we went to work. Of course, you know the capacity of the tent is: one man—crowded, two men—one too many, three men—a miracle and four men—impossible. Nels had to go to work at midnight so the three of us stayed up until he went to work then somehow we managed to get to sleep.[4]

The fire brought forward heroes as well as tragedy. Second Lt. Guy Haskins received a special commendation for saving heavy equipment. Warrant Officer JG Cecil Cutler was recognized for rousing many sleeping men. And Sgt. Stephen Matricciani was singled out for his valiant efforts in saving property and human life.

In early April the battalion received tents from Saidpur to relieve the overcrowding. The men had been sleeping eight to a tent since the fire, and these emergency arrangements were getting old. The soldier railroaders made due with scant aid and relief and were disheartened by a lack of assistance from the American Red Cross.

13

Mutaguchi's Gift

General Mutaguchi prayed to regain the honor he believed he had lost. In early 1943 he had been embarrassed and provoked by Wingate, who had successfully negotiated the terrain that Mutaguchi had earlier reported to the Imperial command was impassable. The Imperial command was developing a plan to invade India. Mutaguchi came to believe that the plan he had dismissed was the emperor's idea, and thus he had disrespected his god-king.[1] The emperor's birthday, April 29, was drawing near, and Mutaguchi was determined that his gift would be India.

In western Burma three divisions of the Imperial Japanese Army massed for a powerful counterattack toward Imphal and Kohima. While Imphal, the main British base in India, was the bigger prize, Kohima was the key to all their plans.

Mutaguchi knew that he couldn't take Imphal so long as the British could resupply it at will. Taking Kohima, a hill town junction about halfway along the 100-mile, north-south route from Dimapur to Imphal, would cut the Allies' supply line. With Kohima secured, the Japanese planned to fight their way up the road to Dimapur, their immediate objective. Lying on the Bengal and Assam Railroad line about 200 miles west of the Ledo terminus and 360 miles east of Parbatipur, Dimapur was a critically important railhead and depot. The supply dump there was a mile wide and eleven miles long and contained everything from dried eggs and potatoes to combat boots and battle tanks.[2]

It was from Dimapur that the Allies supplied both the British base at Imphal and the U.S. and Chinese forces farther north. At the time the railroad was in the capable hands of the U.S. Army's 745th Railway Operating Battalion. With control of Dimapur the entire Brahmaputra Valley and all the Allied air supply bases and

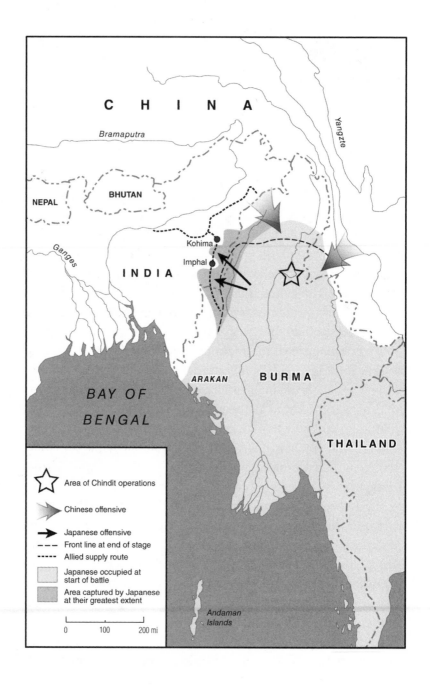

MAP 4. Japanese attack on Imphal and Kohima, March–July 1944. Map by Erin Greb.

combat aircraft operations would be vulnerable. With control of Dimapur the Japanese could knock out the entire Allied supply effort in the China-Burma-India theater. Its capture was imperative for the Japanese conquest of India.

From Dimapur Mutaguchi planned to advance down the Bengal and Assam Railroad, through Parbatipur all the way to Calcutta. He was counting on independence-minded supporters among the Indian population to rise against the Allies, sabotage their lines of communication, and swell the ranks of the Indian National Army.

Once in control of Calcutta, the Japanese would rule all of India. With the Allies out of India, China would sign a separate peace with Japan and isolate the United States in the region. A pacified China would free nearly two million battle-hardened Japanese troops for deployment in other theaters.

But first the Japanese had to take Kohima.

14

The Battle of Kohima

The village of Kohima lay at a sharp westerly turn in the road from Imphal to Dimapur about forty-six miles from the Bengal and Assam railhead. The tidy village of neat bungalows and proper red roofs rested nearly a mile up the mountain but was surrounded by even higher peaks. To the west the mountains rose to nearly 10,000 feet, and to the north and east nearly 8,000.[1] Through this natural passage lay the best and perhaps only way between Assam, with its lines of communication to Calcutta, Manipur, and the stores-laden base at Imphal, and the Japanese main force in Burma.

The British had guessed Mutaguchi's plan and bombed the Japanese columns relentlessly. But just as relentlessly the Japanese kept coming. Mutaguchi's troops marched for twenty days over five mountain ranges with ridges reaching 8,000 feet to get into position for battle.[2] Now, in the first week of April 1944, the Japanese methodically attacked the strong points and hilltops surrounding Kohima from three directions and forced the isolated British and Indian soldiers to withdraw into tighter and tighter defensive positions. The British were run off all but one hilltop approximately two miles from the main garrison. By the end of the siege the garrison's defenders would be packed into an area of only 350 square yards, a godforsaken piece of bombed and burned real estate smaller than a basketball court. They were close enough to throw canteens to each other, which became a practical necessity as the noose tightened around them.

On April 3, still cloaked in early morning darkness, the advance guard platoon of Eleventh Company, Third Battalion, Fifty-eighth Infantry Regiment, and Thirty-first Division of the Imperial Japanese Army reached the outskirts of Naga Village, a mile north of Kohima. The platoon's commander, Kobayashi Naoji, disregarded orders from

Company HQ to take a break and get some sleep. Instead, as daylight began to lighten the hillside, he scouted ahead to determine which fork in the road would be best for his platoon's advance.

Kobayashi spotted British defenders who seemed completely unaware of the Japanese presence. The young commander returned to rouse his platoon and reported what he had seen to his company commander, who ordered all platoons to converge on Kobayashi's position. They obeyed with the stealth their many months in the jungle had taught them. The defenders were taken by surprise, and thus began the Battle for Kohima.

Kobayashi was the first Japanese soldier into Kohima, an honor he relished. But just as rare a feat was the fact that he lived to tell about it. The odds were less than one in four that he would make it back across the Chindwin River into Burma alive.[3]

. . .

Lord Mountbatten had recognized the threat to Dimapur. To counter it he ordered XXXIII Indian Corps into the Assam Valley to secure the road to Imphal. On April 5, 161st Brigade of Fifth Division left Dimapur for Kohima led by the Fourth Royal West Kents. About 500 West Kents made it to Kohima before the Japanese established their ring around it. The trailing elements of 161st Brigade organized a defense on the hilltop of Jotsoma, about two miles to the west, the only elevation the British would control for the two-week siege that was now upon them.

The Japanese pounded Kohima with artillery firing from the surrounding heights throughout the daylight hours. Then, under cover of darkness, the emperor's warriors advanced toward the dug-in defenders using human wave attacks, one wave following another for hours. The defenders, who mowed them down with machine guns and rifles, mortars and grenades, came to call these attacks "pigeon shoots," but the Japanese kept coming. Always the fighting ended in hand-to-hand combat with pistols, knives, bayonets, and bare knuckles. Often the Japanese would gain a few yards at night and the British and Indian soldiers would take them back in the daytime, only to have the bloody cycle repeated a few hours later.

The stench of the dead and dying grew overwhelming. The wounded were being wounded again, a second and third time. Some of the wounded defenders began asking for their pistol as final insurance that, should Kohima be overrun, they would not be used for bayonet practice, the standard Japanese employment for wounded captives.

The defenders began the siege with good stores of food and ammunition, but neither would count for much when the water ran out. A pipe that ran up into the hills supplied the garrison's water, and the Japanese would all too soon control the hills. The pipe was sure to be cut. The Indian General Hospital and Field Supply Depot sections of Kohima both had canvas water tanks that should have been buried but had been left above ground. These were quickly riddled by Japanese bullets.

In the early morning of April 7 the Japanese clawed their way up the ridge and cut off the water supply to the defenders. To make matters worse, the troops defending the ridge, disoriented and dazed, withdrew toward Dimapur instead of Kohima.

As the siege wore on, the defenders' position shrank into an ever more concentrated ring of desperation. Soldiers fought without sleep and with fleeting hope. Supplies and ammo were dropped by parachute, and water was pumped into automobile tire inner tubes for dead drops. But with the perimeter winnowing away these supplies just as often landed in the hands of the enemy instead.[4] The first drop on April 13 was a disaster, as air crews misidentified the recovery zone amid the rugged ridgelines.[5] The Japanese soldiers called their captured food "Churchill rations." By any name it was manna from heaven.

The Royal Air Force quickly remedied the problem. Usually late in the afternoon half a dozen Dakotas flew in tandem through the misty, smoke-filled valleys then circling Garrison Hill. Their color-coded parachutes wafted from the fuselage doors like silky angels descending from heaven and gave brief but welcome comfort to the defenders.

The trees around the defenders, long since burned and stripped of leaves by the relentless artillery barrage, now stood with charred trunks and tortured limbs, their ashen skeletons draped with parachutes. At dusk and dawn they looked like a picket of giant billowing ghosts. It was at just such times that the Japanese would call to the defenders, "Tommy, Tommy, put down your rifle and come have some cool water and beef," or "Tommy, Tommy, your girl back home is lying with a Yank tonight."

The defenders discovered a piped spring northwest of the main garrison, but the spigot was within fifty yards of enemy lines. The defenders could approach only under cover of darkness and then only one at a time. Even with this new source, water rations were reduced to less than a pint a day, with a little more apportioned to the wounded.[6]

On April 17 the battle saw the closest combat imaginable when the grounds around the former home of the district commissioner were contested. The house itself had been leveled by bombardment and only a single chimney remained standing. In what had been a pleasant and pastoral garden just two weeks earlier, opposing armies now dug in on either side of the commissioner's tennis court. The lobbing this time was done not by polite Europeans in scrubbed white shorts but by desperate men in tattered uniforms, volleying with live grenades.

The West Kents defending the Field Supply Depot were spent and needed to be relieved. Two platoons of Assam Rifles and Assam Regiment moved in and took over the Kents' beleaguered positions. But the Japanese had concentrated their forces, and by dark the Indian units were forced to retreat after parrying several assaults. However, the Japanese failed to press the attack, and the brave defenders continued to hold their ground against all odds. In a few hours dawn broke and with it came the faintest glimmer of hope. On the same day the 721st Railway Operating Battalion was being pummeled into submission and made homeless by a violent rain and wind storm, their second humbling in less than a month, the winds of fate finally blew favorably on Kohima's defenders. The 161st Brigade sent a tank detachment and the 1/1st Punjab Battalion to relieve Kohima.

The dauntless Punjabis first secured Hospital Ridge, where 300 wounded awaited evacuation along with dozens of dazed noncombatants. Then they pushed their advance to the district commissioner's bungalow. By April 20 the garrison had been fully relieved, and the Siege of Kohima had reached its bloody conclusion.

But the Battle of Kohima had just begun.

15

After the Storm

On April 18 at 2130 hours, a fierce rain and wind storm fell on the makeshift camp of the 721st Railway Operating Battalion that had risen on landscape scorched by fire less than a month before. The deluge ravaged and destroyed the few remaining bashas and leveled the tents as though they were made of matchsticks and tissue.

The men of the 721st spent that night outdoors in the torrential rain, a precursor to the approaching monsoon, thankful only that no one had been injured or killed. And this time they were thankful too that the destruction was undeniably a result of nature, or perhaps a vengeful Hindu god, but most reassuringly not the work of an enemy.

In the morning they regrouped once more. What else could they do? They couldn't give up and go home, nor did they want to.

As an immediate solution to their dispossession the Battalion Headquarters and Post Exchange moved to the European Institute at Parbatipur. H&S Company again moved in with the pipeliners of the 776th, as did the trackmen of Company C. Company B moved to passenger coaches and boxcars on the dead line at the locomotive shed. The dead line is where locomotives that are not in service are stored, awaiting repair or transfer. In this case, the locomotive facility was used for coaches and boxcars. It was decided then and there that this time the new camp housing would be four-person tents built on concrete floors with six-inch sidewalls. All agreed that the rickety bamboo bashas were simply too great a fire hazard.

By May 1 supplies had started to arrive and construction was slowly getting under way. Most of Company B was still living in the coaches and boxcars on the dead line of the loco shed. The company would tough it out in the boxcars until August.

Payroll too was disrupted. Enlisted men received only partial pay while they awaited H&S Company's reconstruction of army personnel records. The beleaguered H&S suffered a big loss when their personnel sergeant major was admitted to the 112th Station Hospital and later returned to the States.

A captain was assigned to oversee the camp's reconstruction in the hope that he could speed the process. But the pieces of this particular puzzle seemed ever changing, and construction was still dragging when the rains came. By late May the monsoon was upon them and the 721st was still living hand to mouth.

But that didn't keep them from railroading. Nothing could keep them from that. That's why they came to India and, by God, that's what they were determined to do. Everybody knew the stakes: if the freight didn't go east, the Japanese would start coming west, down the very railroad they were running.

16

Inbound

Calcutta was an American port in 1944. It had evolved into the lynchpin of U.S. supply efforts throughout CBI. Its forty-nine berths were continually occupied, and forty-four more ships were typically anchored in the stream.[1] Men worked twelve- to eighteen-hour shifts, twenty-four hours a day, year-round. Its ascension to this pivotal role was unforeseen, but as the war with Japan played out and the Allies regained initiative in the theater, the importance of Calcutta's port became obvious, and the U.S. Army assigned two specialized port battalions, the 497th and the 508th, to secure the docks and run the operation.[2]

Native workers like soldierly ants swarmed below towering gantries, their portage of rough-hewn wooden crates hoisted in precarious suspense. Some wore loose pants, some sarongs, and some simply folded and tucked cloth around their bony hips like bulbous diapers. Most were bare-chested. On a few, sweat-stained, impossibly soiled shirts hung over lean frames of sinew and muscle. All wore a sort of working man's turban, piled and folded on the top of their head to pad their heavy loads. This sweaty, ragged halo of worn cloth was the only thing in their lives that brought them comfort.

Mixed with the immediate stench of the toiling masses and petroleum fumes from the dockside machinery lolled the chronic pall of burning cow dung. This ever-present smell overhung the lowlands of the Ganges-Brahmaputra Delta and clung to its waterfront like fetid gauze. Unwelcome and foul to anyone who had known better in life it was nevertheless the tang of home fires burning in Calcutta.

The laborers in their thousands were dark-skinned and illiterate, many refugees from the famine in Bengal. Their lot in life was an infinitesimal step above that of beasts of burden. Their caste dictated that life would be ever so, and they struggled to avoid letting their shadows fall on other Hindus of higher order lest they suffer a beating for their imposition.

As they shuffled barefoot on the concrete docks, the calluses on their soles thicker than the leather on the GIs' boots, the giant steel skeletal arms of the cranes swung slowly overhead, fetching and lowering, gathering and lifting pallets from the dock to the waiting decks and vice versa. The ghat's choreography was at once mesmerizing and terrifying, a dance of determined danger on a stilted stage.

Amid the throng white MPs assisted by tall Anglo-Indian *jemadar* quartermasters (the lowest ranked junior commissioned officers, approximately a second lieutenant in U.S. Army rank) directed the flow of humanity and motorized traffic. African American GIs drove trucks and dock tugs, hauling and towing everything from food and ammunition to medical supplies as well as that which creates the need for medical attention.

17

Material Inferiority

General Mutaguchi, or more accurately, his men were feeling the pinch in May 1944, for many small reasons that added up to one big one: supplies. Military historians call the cause of their undoing "material inferiority." The Battle for Burma boiled down to an elemental problem. Even if Mutaguchi's troops had carried out their assignments flawlessly, a proposition that neither side could claim, the Japanese still would have lost because they could not resupply their forces in what became a battle of attrition. When the British denied them a quick victory at Kohima and then Imphal, the Japanese attackers were doomed.

The three divisions making up Mutaguchi's Fifteenth Army were a formidable force, but even from the beginning of his campaign to invade India they were not at full strength. In contrast the British IV Corps defending Imphal included three full-strength divisions, a parachute brigade, and a tank brigade. Just as important, the British could rely on reinforcements. Between Dimapur and Kohima the British had two divisions, one infantry corps, and four special brigades that could be relieved and reinforced during battle. Mutaguchi's forces were on their own. They could not be reinforced; they had no air support to speak of, no tanks, and not enough artillery. The British at Imphal received about 500 tons of supplies per day, which meant they could fly their fighters and bombers and transport planes, use their tanks, and batter the Japanese with their artillery before they sent their men forward to attack.[1]

Air power was a huge problem for the Japanese; they simply couldn't compete. In the spring of 1942 they had roamed the skies freely over Burma, threatened only by the brave but vastly outnumbered Americans of the Flying Tigers.

Their commander, Claire L. Chennault, had a long history in

China. In 1937, as a retired captain in the U.S. Army Air Corps, he traveled there at the invitation of Madame Chiang Kai-shek to review and critique that country's air force. By 1941 Chennault was in charge of the American Volunteer Group, a unit of retired Army Air Corps personnel unofficially serving in China. These bold flyers were soon dubbed "the Flying Tigers" and, after the attack on Pearl Harbor, reincorporated into U.S. forces as the Fourteenth Air Force.

By the spring of 1944, the tables had turned. The Japanese could put into the air on average only 41 fighters a day and very few bombers, whereas the Allies launched an average of 480 fighters, 224 bombers, and 31 reconnaissance planes a day.[2]

Air superiority meant the Allies could attack at will during daylight hours. They sank Japanese river supply crafts, riddled trucks, and blew up railroad trains. They bombed Japanese administrative outposts and played havoc with lines of communication. As a result the Japanese could move supplies only at night and then only after they had repaired damaged infrastructure, recordkeeping, and transport. For the Allies it was a different story; the petroleum, spare parts, and powder that made things go *boom*—when and where the Allies wanted—had been dutifully brought forward to airfields and depots on the railroad. And getting that done had been no small task.

. . .

Gen. Miyazaki Shigesaburo, the leader of the Japanese forces at Kohima, was a tough son of a bitch, and his men were no different. His Fifty-eighth Infantry Regiment, although they had been unable to stop the relief of Kohima, still controlled the heights and ridges and strong points throughout the area. They would have to be blown out, bayoneted out, and burned out of every bunker, cave, and trench before the road to Imphal could be reopened.

The British deployed a brigade north of Kohima to shut down Miyazaki's supply line from the Chindwin. At some point over the next two months the provisions Mutaguchi had sent with his troops ran out. Calorie deficits became more lethal than bullets, as Japanese soldiers began to die of hunger by the hundreds.

With starvation came dissension. Very little in the way of food and supplies reached the Japanese after the British moved to cut their lines. The most isolated was Thirty-first Division, the force attacking Kohima. Their line of communication was impossibly long. The disciplined and courageous "super warriors of the jungle" began to throw down their arms, fight over food, argue, and disobey direct orders. Transport of provisions and supplies became impossible when over 17,000 horses and mules perished for lack of food.[3]

Lt. Gen. Sato Kotoku commanded the doomed division. In a prescient moment on the eve of battle more than a month earlier, he had toasted his assembled officers with a glass of champagne at his divisional headquarters in the jungle west of Maungaing. His words were direct: "I'll take the opportunity, gentlemen, of making something quite clear to you. Miracles apart, every one of you is likely to lose his life in this operation. It isn't simply a question of the enemy's bullets. You must be prepared for death by starvation in these mountain fastnesses."[4] And so they died.

After ten weeks of battle, "shedding bitter tears," Sato defied Mutaguchi and disengaged his forces.[5] The prophetic general could take no more. He had watched his troops scrounge for food like starving vermin and attempt to do battle with dwindling ammunition and no hope for support. To fight further would mean certain annihilation, so he quit.[6]

It was the end of the Japanese invasion of India and the beginning of the end of the Japanese conquest of Burma. The fighting would still be long and bloody, but the tide had turned. The fighting for Imphal and Kohima made casualties of 65,000 Japanese and 16,700 British, Indian, and Gurkha soldiers.[7] Lord Mountbatten said of the fighting at Kohima, "It was probably one of the greatest battles in history . . . in effect the Battle of Burma . . . naked unparalleled heroism. . . . [It was] the British-Indian Thermopylae."[8]

Years later, after the artillery smoke had dissolved into the mountain ether and the florid, lush jungle engulfed the stench of rotting corpses, it could be said that the Japanese lost not because of the men they brought to battle but because of the matériel they couldn't bring.[9]

18

Monsoon

With the monsoon nearly upon them the men of the 721st walked
back and forth to work, seven days a week, in utter misery. They
tried wearing rubber boots, but the water was too deep and the
boots filled with the muddy mix that overflowed the rice paddies
and sloshed and gurgled as they walked. The men were wet all
the time. When the sun came out they baked. It was so humid that
vapor rose from the drenched countryside like the steam rising in
their well-maintained boilers. Their clothes and shoes rotted within
days. Blankets and bedding stayed damp and mildewed with no
opportunity to dry. The smell of decay was all around. Conditions
were so miserable that just finding a dry space and paper and pen
to write a letter home—to tell your family and loved ones you were
okay, though you really weren't—proved to be a major undertaking.

The food was bad and the prickly heat tormenting. Mosquitoes
and flies were but two of many species that made nights seem like
the GIs were in India simply to provide a buffet for insects. Par-
asites came in all forms. More advanced organisms like leeches
and ticks were visible and removable, but just as predacious were
the bacteria, fungi, and microbes that invisibly invaded a man's
body to feed off its flesh or blood.

It was in these, the early days of his first monsoon, that Jim
Hantzis reported an initial outbreak of jungle rot, a scaly growth
on his lower right leg. Scores of other GIs reported the same. The
disease was caused by a virus that would lie dormant, then activate at random intervals. Crusty scales would manifest in the same
spot on Hantzis's leg, neither migrating nor spreading and lasting
for maybe two or three weeks. He treated it with a generic topi-
cal ointment. Jungle rot had no recognized cure save for a black
walnut tincture that gained credence through the unofficial CBI

grapevine. But either Hantzis didn't know about this remedy or it failed him because whatever was eating at him would find him a convenient host for the rest of his life.

The rain, of course, flooded the tracks and made railroading miserable too. It washed away the ballast and dislodged ties; loose ties allowed rails to give way under the weight of trains. Picking up after a wreck was another one of Company B's responsibilities.

If a train derails in a small way—say, one wheel of one car falls off a rail—the typical rerailing procedure involves the use of blocks of wood and jacking. The wood is cut into pieces, usually around two feet in length, and formed in the shape of a wedge; as the car is slowly pulled forward or shoved backward, these wedges, one stacked atop another, raise the wheel to the height of the rail. During this operation men use their bare hands to place the wedges exactly where they need them, inches from the moving wheel, and if all goes right, the wheel slides back onto the rail and everybody agrees to go slow over the bad section of track until it can be repaired.

Another approach is to jack up the car and rebuild the rail under it. Again, in a small wreck you can get away with using blocks and jacks, but in a big wreck involving many overturned cars and really badly damaged equipment, you need a steam crane, also called a hook car, to do the job right. The big problem for the 721st and especially the men of Company B was that the only hook car available was a thirty-ton broad-gauge unit. If a wreck happened on a metre-gauge line, unless the broad-gauge line ran nearby, the work had to be done manually with blocks and jacks and such.

It goes without saying that the wreck crew was not a crew the men looked forward to working. Wrecks were hard enough to deal with in daylight on a nice day. As the men of the 721st were finding out, Dante had nothing on CBI when it came to conjuring hell. If India was Limbo, Burma was Satan's true playground.

19

The Siege of Myitkyina

The Allies had their own dream: to push the Japanese out of northern Burma and simultaneously advance across central Burma toward Rangoon. The Japanese had bitten off more than they could chew. General Mutaguchi's mistaken reliance on willpower over resupply doomed his attack on Imphal, ruined his chance of taking India, and ultimately cost the Japanese Burma. Mutaguchi ordered 150,000 troops into the wilds with rations for only two weeks; he was certain they would filter through jungles, cross rivers, climb mountains, capture Imphal, and there feast on hors de combat from the British depot. He was wrong, and his men began starving and running out of ammunition soon after they failed to cut the supply line to Imphal at Kohima in June 1944.

. . .

Throughout early 1944 General Stilwell had been making progress moving down the Hukawng Valley with his Chinese forces toward the town of Myitkyina and its vital airstrip. With Myitkyina secure the Allies would be able to move supplies to China via the Ledo Road, hampered only by Burma's natural impedimenta.

To the eastern and southern flanks of the retreating Japanese, Merrill's Marauders were proving to be as tough as advertised. On the logistical front the American railroaders, brave air crews, truck drivers, and road builders were seeing to it that vital supplies kept coming in ever-increasing amounts.

The British, under the leadership of thirty-nine-year-old Gen. Orde Wingate, were keeping up their end of the offensive undeterred by sentiment in their high command to skip Burma altogether. Gen. Sir William Slim—the man who would ultimately liberate Burma—wrote, "Wingate was a strange, excitable, moody

creature, but he had a fire in him. He could ignite other men."[1]
The unorthodox commando chief was intent on maintaining a
rather orthodox fixed base in the thick of enemy-occupied territory 200 miles from friendly support. From this position, complete
with a makeshift airstrip, he planned to muster 10,000 troops and
launch an ambitious drive to cut the Mandalay–Myitkyina Railroad, a Japanese lifeline.

In mid-March Wingate succeeded, severing the rail line supplying Myitkyina at Mawlu, eighty miles to the south. This left
Myitkyina without its main line of communication and meant
that most of the matériel necessary for resupply had to move up
the Irrawaddy River, a slower, less dependable, and more dangerous route.

Sadly Wingate would not see the successful conclusion of the war
in Burma. After visiting British headquarters at Imphal on the evening of March 24, he ignored concerns of his U.S. Air Commando
bomber crew and boarded a B-25 Mitchell to return to Burma. He
and the entire crew were killed when the plane flew into a hillside
in a violent storm sometime around midnight.

Stilwell read the situation correctly. He knew that if he could
press the attack before Mutaguchi regrouped, the Allies could
take control of Myitkyina. The main thrust of Stilwell's offensive,
code-named Operation End Run, would come from the Marauu-
ers executing a wide flanking move to the east and attacking first
the airfield, then the town of Myitkyina. A supporting feint would
come from the Chinese Sixty-fifth Regiment and Chinese Twenty-
second Division.

But before any attack could proceed, Stilwell needed to replen-
ish the worn and depleted Marauders, who were now less than half
of their original number since starting out in February.[2] He reinforced the American fighters with Chinese and Burmese and reorganized them into three battalions, dubbed the H, K, and M Forces.

On April 27 General Merrill issued orders to move out. H and K
Forces were to move from Naubum to Taikri, then head east along
the main Kumon Range before turning south to Ritpong. From
there they were to advance south to the edge of the Myitkyina

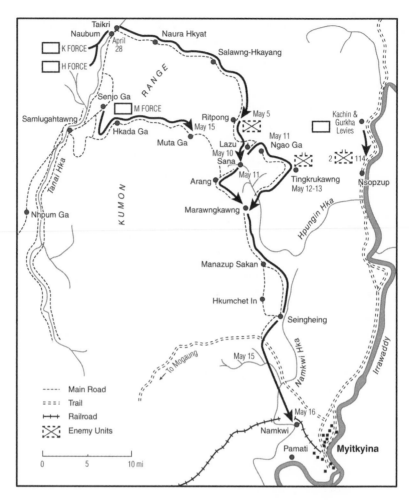

MAP 5. Merrill's Marauders, 5307th Composite Unit (Provisional), campaign to retake Myitkyina, February–August 1944. Map by Erin Greb.

plain. M Force was to operate to the south of H and K and block any Japanese attempt to intercept the other two columns during the first stage of the advance.

The first challenge for the men and mules of the newly reinforced Marauders was to cross the Kumon Mountain Range. These saw-toothed ridges descend south from the border with China and contain among their wonders Burma's highest peak, Mount Hkakabo, at 19,296 feet. The Marauders would transit at Naura Hkyat,

6,100 feet high, mud-slicked and overgrown.[3] The narrow trail, which hadn't been used in ten years, clung to the steep mountainside like ivy to a tree trunk.[4] Unforgiving cliff faces loomed around every twist in the path. According to the unit's native Kachin guides, it would be impossible to cross even in the best weather. Stilwell said it had to be done.

The Marauders had battled the trail for nearly six days when their godawful journey revealed the coming fight. Upon reaching Naura Hkyat, an I&R platoon reported back that the eastern flank of the Chinese regiment attached to K Force had brushed with the Japanese at the village of Ritpong, directly in the Marauder's path. The enemy was believed to be holding the town in considerable strength. There was no way around the village, so K Force would have to take it.

The Japanese decided to retreat to the south, toward Myitkyina, and promptly found themselves in the jaws of the Marauders' crossfire. The fleeing Japanese used smoke grenades as a screen, but their losses were heavy. By May 9 K Force had secured the village. The next day it was decided that the Chinese should stay and mop up the area and that the Marauders of K Force should continue south.

During the four days that K Force spent clearing Ritpong, H Force caught up with them and moved ahead. But on May 10 both units were at the village of Lazu, roughly thirty-five miles north of Myitkyina. To the east of Lazu, about twenty miles away, the British-led Gurkhas and Kachins were stalled by considerable Japanese resistance in their drive to Nsopzup. It was decided that H Force would continue the advance toward Myitkyina and K Force would make a feint toward Nsopzup to draw the Japanese away from the Gurkhas and Kachins and protect H Force's eastern flank.

While K Force kept the Japanese busy around Ritpong, H Force advanced toward Myitkyina. As they moved southward they were met by a guide from Detachment 101, a Kachin trained by the Office of Strategic Services (OSS), the forerunner of the Central Intelligence Agency. Here, north of Myitkyina, where secrecy and surprise were paramount, the OSS provided local intelligence. It was their operatives who would see to it that the Marauders stayed on the proper trail through an unmarked jumble of pathways as they executed the final phase of their approach.

On May 16 H Force crossed the Namkwi River south of a village by the same name. This placed the Marauders only four miles from Myitkyina's airfield. The attack began at 1000 hours the next morning. By 1100 hours the ferry terminal was in the hands of the Marauders, and by noon the Chinese 150th Regiment had taken the airfield. Sporadic fighting flared for the rest of the day, but the Allies easily maintained control of their objectives and advanced even farther southeast toward the Irrawaddy River. Colonel Hunter radioed Merrill with the coded message "The Merchant of Venice": the airstrip was secure and the runway usable.

But in this swift victory lay the seed of a much longer engagement. When the Japanese did not quickly reinforce their positions nor mount a significant counterattack at the airfield on May 17, Colonel Hunter surmised that enemy troop strength in the town of Myitkyina was low. He was right. But could he keep the Japanese out? Hunter decided H Force should attack before the Japanese could reinforce. Therefore blocking enemy reinforcements became the indispensable key to his strategy since there were thousands of Japanese soldiers in the surrounding area.

Hunter set an attack on the city and its main access routes for the next morning. Two battalions of the Chinese 150th were designated for the assault on Myitkyina, and another was to be kept in reserve. White Combat Team of H Force would be sent south of the city to secure a ferry crossing; Red Combat Team was to continue to hold the crossing at Pamati, thus blocking two of the three approaches to the city from the south.

Soon General Merrill had Myitkyina cut off from reinforcements in all directions save due east, across the swollen Irrawaddy. The airfield was functional and supplies were arriving amid sporadic small arms fire. Merrill's ring around Myitkyina was solid but not impenetrable. The Japanese snuck back in; between 3,000 and 4,000 infiltrated via Nsopzup, Mogaung, and Bhamo. They built

FIG. 1. Christmas 1944. Sergeants James Hantzis, Les Gruseck, William Newman, and Earl Whittaker.

FIG. 2. In 1926, twenty years after emigrating to the United States from Chomori, Greece, Nick and Harry Hantzis opened the Hantzis Bros. Restaurant in the Lorraine Hotel near Union Station in Indianapolis. James Hantzis, my father, is the young man in the foreground. James's father, Harry, is to his right.

FIG. 3. On June 23, 1943, six months before leaving for India, James Harry Hantzis married Mary Louise (Marilou) Mount, a registered nurse from Greensburg, Indiana.

FIG. 4. Camp Cushing, three miles south of Fort Sam Houston in San Antonio, Texas. The 721st Railway Operating Battalion received technical training here through the hot summer months of 1943 prior to deployment to India. The battalion was quartered in tarpaper shanties next to the Southern Pacific's double main line.

FIG. 5. 721st Railway Operating Battalion (ROB), Camp Cushing, Texas, June 1943. Photo courtesy of U.S. Army.

FIG. 6. The Brass Rail Bar, Moonbeam Murphy, proprietor. Camp Cushing, Texas, 1943.

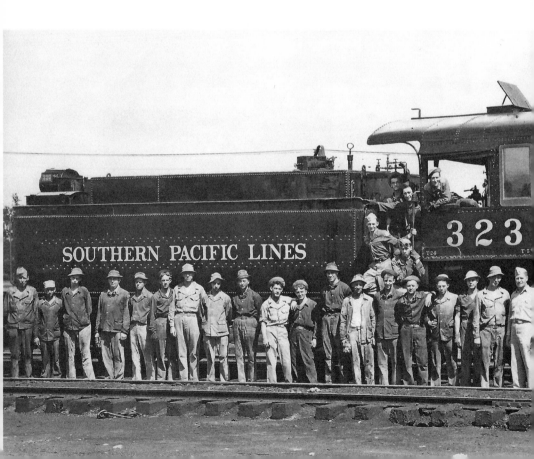

FIG. 7. A shoe-shine boy outside the gate of Camp Cushing, Texas, 1943.

FIG. 8. Technical training, Camp Cushing, Texas, July 1943.
Photo courtesy of U.S. Army.

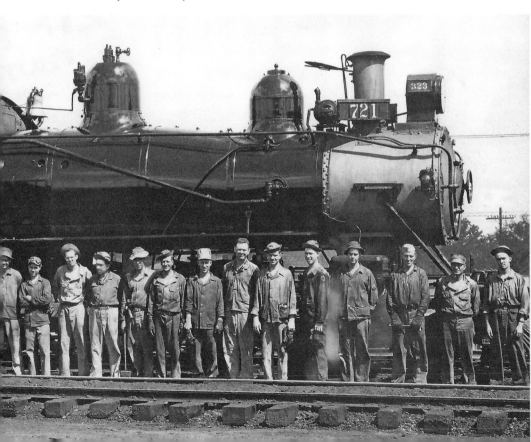

FIG. 9. (*Opposite top*) Technical
training, locomotive driver repair,
Camp Cushing, Texas, July 1943.
Photo courtesy of U.S. Army.

FIG. 10. (*Opposite bottom*) Technical
training, locomotive boiler repair,
Camp Cushing, Texas, July 1943.
Photo courtesy of U.S. Army.

FIG. 11. (*Above*) Crows on a wire.
Far left, Pvt. George Lee, Company
B, 721st ROB, Kansas City, Kansas.
Third from left, S.Sgt. James Hantzis,
Company B, 721st ROB, Indianapolis,
Indiana. Shop Yards, Parbatipur, State
of Bengal, India, 1945. The boxcars
in the background are where the GIs
slept after the camp fire.

FIG. 12. Hitler under guard, captured by Company B. Left to right: Tech 4 Charles Brothers, Lake View, Michigan, no railroad affiliation; Pvt. Joe Ward, off the L&N from Birmingham, Alabama; S.Sgt. Romelo Pavia, New York City; Pvt. Tobias Olson, West Willmar, Minnesota, off the Great Northern; Tech 5 Stewart White, Wood, California, off the Southern Pacific.

FIG. 13. S.Sgt. Matthew Appel, Company B, 721st ROB, with a tiger cub, Parbatipur, State of Bengal, India, 1944.

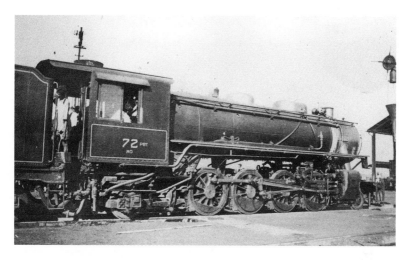

FIG. 14. Engine No. 72, Parbatipur yards.

FIG. 15. A thirty-ton, broad-gauge steam wrecker crane, Parbatipur yards, 1944.

FIG. 16. A thirty-ton crane at a twenty-eight-car wreck, May 1945. The wreck involved ammunition, blasting powder, bombs, and shells. Engineer E. O. Woods from North Syracuse, New York, worked this wreck for twenty-three hours.

FIG. 17. Camp fire, March 25, 1944, Parbatipur, State of Bengal, India. All the tents burned and all personnel records were destroyed. The battalion was without permanent quarters for months but never stopped railroading.

FIG. 18. The rebuilt Parbatipur Camp, 1945.

FIG. 19. Parbatipur Camp Saluting Area, 1945.

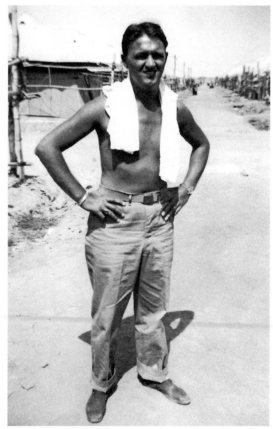

FIG. 20. (*Opposite top*) Parbatipur
Camp road, 1945.

FIG. 21. (*Opposite bottom*) S.Sgt. James
H. Hantzis, Company B, 721st ROB,
Parbatipur, 1945.

FIG. 22. (*above*) Parbatipur
North Yards, 1944.

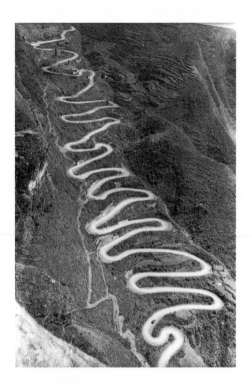

FIG. 23. Ledo Road, showing the twenty-one curves of the Kunming-Kweilin section. Photo courtesy of U.S. Army.

FIG. 24. Indian guard, Parbatipur timber yard, 1944.

up their strength, consolidated their forces, and by May 23 they were shifting from defense to offense.

The Americans too were exhausted, but Stilwell ordered that evacuation of the ill and wounded be kept to an "absolute minimum." Orders even went out to the Marauders' base camp at Dinjan, India, thirty-two miles west of Ledo, to immediately forward every capable convalescent to Burma. A unit of 2,600 American replacements that had just arrived in India for training at Ramgarh was rushed to the front lines. Many of these green troops, although paired with experienced Marauders, simply couldn't take it; conditions in Burma were incomprehensible and the style of fighting induced debilitating shock. Roughly fifty of the new recruits and officers were soon classified as psychopathic cases.[5]

Also rushed in were GIs from the 209th Engineer Combat Battalion, a light construction outfit designed to repair runways and quickly build combat roads and bridges. These troops were given twenty-four hours' notice. They immediately packed their things, discontinued their operation of gravel and ice plants in India, and boarded transport planes to Myitkyina.[6]

Even men from the U.S. railway battalions were sent to Myitkyina. Most of the 160 soldiers who were detailed there were good men, but some of the "volunteers" were later described as men who were in trouble with their battalion brass, men for whom Myitkyina was an alternative to disciplinary action. Whatever their circumstances, once in Myitkyina they were designated the Sixty-first Composite Group and dutifully and courageously operated Jeep trains, sometimes called "bailing-wire cannonballs," over the thirty-one miles of railroad between Myitkyina and Mogaung.[7]

The Sixty-first Composite Group had to use Jeeps for power because the Japanese had buried the flat rods—the rods connecting the pistons to the drive wheels—of all but a couple of the captured locomotives. So the resourceful GIs got busy replacing the wheels on armed Jeeps with rims from six-wheel-drive GMC trucks, which fit the track gauge perfectly. Then they chained two Jeeps together and pulled two or maybe three flatcars loaded with troops, pipeline supplies, oil, and gas. GIs rode the flatcars to apply the handbrakes because the trusty little Jeeps had no stopping power.[8]

Whatever the motivation might have been of those so quickly thrown together, the hasty reinforcement of the Allies with "any man who could hold a rifle" was all that prevented the Japanese from overrunning the airstrip. Still the Japanese maintained positions only 1,500 yards away, and during the last days of May they succeed in littering the runway with disabled aircraft and stalling the Allied resupply efforts.

The siege of Myitkyina went on through June and July. On August 1 Gen. Mizukami Genzo, the commander of Japanese forces, sent to relieve Myitkyina, realized that he and Col. Maruyama Husayasu, commander of the garrison, would not be able to hold the city and that Myitkyina could not be reinforced. The general released his soldiers to evacuate any way they could. He then made apologies to his emperor and committed suicide.

The vestiges of America's first special operations forces joined the final attack on August 3, 1944. When the town was secured at 1545 hours it was said, then and forever, that the Marauders had kicked the Japanese out of Myitkyina. Burma may have driven the Marauders to the edge of oblivion, but it was the Japanese who fell into the abyss.

20

A Ghost in the Yards

The muted report of the blast left less of an impression than seeing what had happened. Jim Hantzis shook his head in momentary disbelief. He couldn't fathom what he had just witnessed. Sure, it was dusk and the shadows in the rail yards further dimmed his view, but it had happened less than fifty yards away. He asked Nels Whittaker, "Did you see that?"

Nels stuck his neck forward, strained his eyes, and shook his head back and forth. Finally he managed to reply, "I saw it, but I ain't believin' it." Then, straining even harder, he said, "On second thought, I didn't see anything! Not a damn thing! They got what they deserved, those slimy little bastards."

It was routine for Parbatipur Yards and its nearby passenger depot to handle Japanese POWs on their way through India to Cowra, a camp in New South Wales, Australia. The prisoners came through in special wooden vans with barred ventilation slits at the top and bottom of all four corners of the coach. What was unusual, however, was the arrival at the same time of the bedraggled remnants of the 5307th Composite, Merrill's Marauders.

The railroaders always managed to muster some good chow when they knew the Marauders were passing through. The 721st even found a few beers as well. And the Marauders were always glad to talk, share smokes, and shoot the breeze with the GI railroaders. But these men were just happy to be alive; most of them were so skinny they looked like they could box featherweight.

What Jim and Nels saw on their way to evening mess was a convenient settling of scores, removed in time, perhaps, but not in mind. Someone slender and lithe—Jim and Nels assumed it was a Marauder—climbed the ladder on the end of a railroad car holding

Japanese prisoners of war, pulled the pin on a grenade, waited two seconds, then slipped it through the bars of the top vent.

The muffled explosion followed, and the car rocked ever so gently just as the grenadier landed like a cat on the gravel ballast of the track bed from halfway down the ladder. Unfazed, he stood up, brushed off his hands, and walked away as though nothing had happened. He never looked back.

After that everybody went about their business.

21

Kaunia Junction

The railroad tracks were a boundary between civilization and the wild. Herb Witt, a Milwaukee Road station master with H&S Company, had taken over for the second-trick block station operator at 2300 hours, but he had been in the two-story wooden structure for about three hours before his third-trick shift catching up on gossip and killing time.[1] That was pretty much the standard routine at Kaunia Junction, halfway between Parbatipur and Lalmanirhat. There wasn't a whole lot to do but fish for catfish in the Tista River, raid the local wine-making operation, and shoot the breeze with fellow GIs. When Herb joined the group a little after 2000 hours that evening a predictable conversation was already under way.

"No, no, the old guy told me that they use meat to start the fermentation. I swear it!" insisted the beefy trackman Dominick Capiello to Reno Nones, the station's medic. Capiello was from Delaware County, New York, and Nones was from Monongahela, Pennsylvania.

Nones scratched his head and asked skeptically, "You're telling me that all they do is stick a hunk of meat down a hole in a bamboo joint, wait a couple weeks, drill a hole at the bottom of the joint, and drain off pure alcohol?"

"Try it yourself," Capiello said with a shrug of his shoulders. "I mix it with orange juice. The natives use some other kind of fruit concoction. Hey, but whatever you drink with it, just be careful—it's potent stuff."

Frank Maloney, the detachment's cook, chimed in, "I'll buy you guys a barrel of the stuff if you leave my wine alone! Hell, every time I get a good batch going, I pull back the cloth to check the vat, and it's already empty! Come on, give a guy a break."

Herb broke into the conversation with a warning: "Frankie, we're just trying to do you a favor and drink up the evidence before you get busted by the Company on a surprise inspection. You think they've forgotten about us out here? You never know when some brass might show up. You're still in hot water from that tiger expedition. What'd the captain tell you? One more stunt like that and you'd be switching cars in Myitkyina."

"Hey, that tiger hunt was a legitimate public affairs operation," shot back the cook. "Hell, the villagers came to us and asked for our help. What're we supposed to do! The book says we're supposed to be considerate of the natives, be friendly. What could be friendlier than shooting a tiger that's been eating their cousins?" When the group's laughter started to fade, he added, "By all rights, they should have gave me a Purple Heart." Then he stood and pulled his shirttail out of his pants and lifted it up to his shoulders. Staring down at his chest, he said, "See what I mean?" and rotated for all to see five long red scars running from his breastbone to his belly button.

Then the laughter started again.

Not long after Herb arrived that evening, an old man so frightfully skinny and frail that he looked as though a strong wind could knock him over appeared at the block station. An Indian train crew removed him from the station platform to the far side of the interlocking, where two tracks intersected, and sat him on a cinderblock at the bottom of the railroad embankment. Since the block station was elevated to give the operator a good view of the approaching traffic, Herb could plainly see where the crew had left him, about thirty yards away. The last Herb remembered of the old man he was rocking gently back and forth, swaying to some inaudible rhythm. Then it was dark.

The night passed uneventfully. The trains came and went and everything ran smoothly. In the late hours of Herb's shift, as the horizon moved ever closer to the rays of the sun, the area surrounding the block station again became visible, sketched in a soft cerise glow and dim morning mist. It was then that he saw the grizzly remains. In the darkness and desolation the old man had been savaged by the scavengers of the night, probably hyenas. As Herb stared through bleary eyes at the ruddy skeleton where once a man had been, vultures and kites arrived to finish the work.

22

Brothers

Rocky Agrusti, a fireman from Selkirk, New York, chuckled at the blue banter that flowed from the mock-serious poker game engaging the two off-duty engine crews of Company C. His time, he thought, might be better spent writing home, but that evening's company was particularly entertaining and the moment light. Besides, he thought there was a better than average chance that he might get called for the Saidpur Extra marked up (scheduled) for 2100 hours. He figured hanging around the loco shed crew area might save him a walk in the rain.

As he leaned against the break room wall, Rocky chatted with Lyle Sanderson, a station master from H&S Company. Lyle, also from New York, told Rocky about visiting his brother, one of four in the service, deep in northern Burma. "He kept writing me these letters telling me that he was coming through India from Karachi and that he'd find me in Parbatipur, and sure enough he did. Then I heard from him, and he was in Ledo getting ready to jump off with one of the engineer battalions."

"Did he tell you where he was going?"

"Nah, he couldn't," replied Lyle. "Classified, you know."

"But you knew he's headed into Burma, right?"

"Right, so I got a couple three-day passes and hitched a ride on a C-47 from up around Lalmanirhat. Turned out that he had gone further into Burma than I thought, and I had to spend a night in the jungle beside some one-lane dirt strip with no lights. The pipeline guys there told me he had moved further east. So we fueled up in the morning and flew on, and I found him damn near to Myitkyina. They were building a pontoon bridge across the Irrawaddy. Boy, you talk about surprised," smiled Lyle.

Just then the door to the break room opened on its squeaky

hinges. Only one of the men looked up from the ring of players cir-cling the barrelhead table when a messenger from H&S Company entered the crew area. The card player gave him only a momen-tary glance. The messenger looked over the crowd, fixed his eyes on Rocky, and waved him toward the door. When Rocky got close enough for no one else to hear, the messenger said, "You're wanted in the first sergeant's office, pronto."

As they prepared to step outside into the early evening darkness and rain, Rocky, thinking he had done something wrong, asked, "What's this about?" The messenger only shrugged and offered the extra poncho he had brought, but Rocky already had one.

As they walked across the muddy rail yards to the Company HQ Rocky mentally reviewed the previous few days and couldn't bring to mind any transgression or foul-up that might warrant a talking-to or discipline. When they arrived at the first sergeant's office he was puzzled to find only the chaplain seated behind the sergeant's desk, reading a letter. In just a matter of seconds Rocky's puzzlement gave way to a heavier mood.

"Rocky," began the chaplain, "are you feeling well, my son?"

"Yes, Father, I feel fine. What's going on?" asked Rocky in a slightly shaky voice.

The chaplain stepped from behind the desk and pointed to a straight-back wooden chair along the wall. Rocky took the seat as requested, and the chaplain asked, "Do you have a brother named Francis, Rocky?"

"Yes, yes I do, Father."

In a calm and sadly reassuring voice the chaplain intoned, "My son, I'm sorry to tell you that your brother Francis was killed in action fighting on Biak Island, New Guinea, this past May."

Rocky was stunned and silent.

The chaplain continued, "Is there anything I can do for you, Rocky? Anyone I can talk to for you or contact?"

Rocky slowly formed two questions in his mind: how did it hap-pen, and did his parents know? Of the two he asked the latter out loud. The chaplain answered, "Yes."

Rocky looked down at the floor for a second, then asked, "My brother Tony's in Africa and my bother Carmen is somewhere at sea. Do they know?"

The chaplain nodded reassuringly and put his right hand on Rocky's shoulder. Then he offered to stay until Rocky felt strong enough to leave the office, but Rocky declined the offer and asked if he might be excused. "Of course, my son," the chaplain said. "May we take a moment to pray before you go?"

Rocky nodded.

The chaplain said a short prayer, then handed Rocky the letter. The men parted company and Rocky returned to his bunk, where he curled into a ball and wept his eyes out before falling asleep after midnight, emotionally exhausted. That night, in his disjointed dreams of his family, he fought a million encounters with death as reconciliation ran like the ghost of his brother before him. It ran farther and farther ahead of the young man, far into the future and far distant from his heart.

. . .

That same night, five time zones to the west, 156,000 men were wide awake and soon to begin their own mortal encounters in a dream from which legions would never awaken. As parachutes snapped open in the darkness over France muted by the throbbing drone of C-47s, the first of their number—for an exquisite instant—were as alive and awake and reconciled as men can ever be. It was June 6, 1944, and the Allies were landing in Europe.

23

Japanese Retrench

On July 3, 1944, General Mutaguchi, finally unable any longer to ignore the obvious, ordered a general retreat for what was left of his battered Fifteenth Army. It was an unnecessary command. What remained of the force that had set out in March on the failed invasion of India was already moving east, that is, the ones who weren't too weak to walk and were left starving in the jungles.

Mutaguchi's losses were so devastating that by October the Imperial General Headquarters had to redraw the entire Burma Area Army's mission. No longer was the goal in Burma to prevent the establishment of communications from India to China. In the face of the Allied offensive the mission was simply to hold southern Burma. And to make the pill all the more bitter, Japanese commanders were told not to expect any additional forces. That left the Japanese with about 100,000 combat troops and 60,000 support troops in Burma.[1]

The redrawing of their mission also left them without Mutaguchi, the divinely inspired commander whose unhappy subordinates quoted him saying, "Lack of weapons is no excuse for defeat." He was relieved and replaced by Lt. Gen. Katamura Shibachi.

The new Japanese plan to hold southern Burma was to make a stand along an east-west line about 350 to 430 miles north of Rangoon. The western anchor of the line was held by the Twenty-eighth Army near the coastal town of Akyab. What remained of Mutaguchi's Fifteenth Army held—in a loose sense of the word—the center around Mandalay along the Irrawaddy River. About 250 miles southeast of Imphal, the Thirty-third Army held the eastern flank near Lashio, about 170 miles south of Myitkyina.

Another new face in CBI, Gen. Kimura Heitaro, now in charge of the entire Burma Area Army, decided not to defend Burma's north. He reasoned that the supply problems the Allies would encounter in their advance on his positions farther south would be to his advantage and his own logistical difficulties would lessen as he fell back closer to his rear bases. The plan was logical and militarily sensible, but not very *bushido*—faithful to the samurai essence. As a consequence Japanese morale continued to suffer.

This new face, Kimura, formerly of the Ordnance Administration Headquarters in Tokyo, would direct not only the Japanese loss of Burma but also, his pet personal project, the construction of a railway from Nong Pladuck in Thailand to Thanbyuzayat in Burma, a distance of 414 kilometers. The Siam–Burma Railway would cost 80,000 to 100,000 civilians and prisoners their lives and inspire the book and movie *The Bridge on the River Kwai*. Along with his many other crimes, building the railway would earn Kimura a capital sentence in the war trials after Japan's surrender, for which he would die in a hangman's noose on December 23, 1948. But in October 1944 he was the shining new star upon whom the Imperial General Headquarters hung their hopes to stanch their losses in Burma.

While Kimura reorganized the Burma Area Army, Lord Mountbatten reorganized the Southeast Asia Command. He selected Lt. Gen. Sir Oliver Leese as the overall commander of Allied land forces in CBI. Along with General Slim's Fourteenth Army and the British XV Corps, Leese would coordinate the Americans under Maj. Gen. Daniel I. Sultan in northern Burma and all Chinese Expeditionary Forces attacking Burma from China.

Lord Mountbatten endorsed a plan to retake Burma by the start of the rainy season, in May 1945. The plan called for the Americans and the Chinese to advance from the north, securing the Ledo Road in the process. At the same time British forces would push southeast from Imphal as well as east from the Arakan coastal area. The plan was to take Mandalay by February, then Rangoon by May.

24

Medic! Medic!

Nick Costello rolled into a ball as he fell, but it was too late. He had felt the boxcar's pin-lifter hit him in the middle of his back, and in the instant before he landed he tried to tuck in his limbs. The blow pushed him forward and knocked him to the ballast. Then a cold sensation unlike any he had ever before experienced ran up his spine. As the cut of cars silently rolled past, the wheel trucks just inches from his face, he lost consciousness.

Don Blair, the second brakeman on that afternoon's No. 4 switch engine crew, saw it all happen. He was twenty car-lengths away manning the ladder switches. At first he started to run toward Nick, but then he thought better of it and ran back toward the engine, ten cars to the rear. As he closed the distance, he cupped his hands to his mouth and yelled in the direction of the cab, "Get a medic! Get a medic! Nick's down! Nick's down! Send the fireman! Do it now! He's hurt! He's hurt!" Between cries for help he made the hand signal for accident—a quick cut of his cupped hand across the side of his thigh.

When he was two cars away from the cab Don saw the engineer lean out the window and give him a thumbs-up to indicate he understood the message. A second later the fireman jumped from the locomotive steps and began running toward the South Yard.

Don saw the engineer wave him toward the accident, so he spun on his heels and began running back toward Nick. It seemed to take forever to cover the distance, every footfall an eternity. Five cars away he began yelling, "Nick! Nick! You okay? Say something, buddy! You okay?" There was no answer. Nick wouldn't be answering anybody that day.

When Don reached Nick he pulled him back from the rail into the space between the two classification tracks, but a part of him didn't follow. Nick's left leg from just below his knee remained between the rails of Track 14. Don couldn't believe his eyes. He came very near to going into shock. Then something deep inside him grabbed control. He remembered his training and began to think of how to administer first aid.

He stood above the unconscious man and stripped his khaki web belt from the loops of his work fatigues. Then he knelt over Nick and tightened the belt above the injury, all the while saying, "You're going to be okay, buddy. Hang in there. Hang in there." After he was sure the tourniquet had stopped the bleeding—Nick had already lost a lot of blood and his color was ashen—Don removed his jacket and folded it into a pillow. He lifted Nick's head, took off his cap, and put the jacket underneath. As he was thinking of what else he might be able to offer the injured man besides a prayer, two corpsmen ran up carrying a folded stretcher. The fireman was close behind them; the engineer had stayed with the engine in case he was needed to move cars.

The lead corpsman cut what was left of Nick's fatigues away from the injury and applied a compression pack to the stump. The second corpsman taped the bandage in place, then they both worked to insert a plasma drip into Nick's left forearm. When they had finished, within ten minutes of their arrival, the lead corpsman elevated the plasma bag and the fireman and second corpsman lifted the stretcher. Carefully but quickly they carried Nick to the Red Cross Jeep that was waiting by the engine on the lead. As they lifted the stretcher, the lead corpsman said to Don, "Good work, soldier. If he makes it, you probably saved his life."

Don just nodded.

As the stretcher departed, Don looked down at the mangled mass of bloody trouser leg and the twisted work boot still containing Nick's foot and part of his leg. For a second he wondered if he should bring it along.

The corpsmen loaded Nick across the hood of the vehicle and secured the stretcher, then drove carefully over the rugged ballast and hump tracks onto a dirt road. Don could see the rear tires of the Jeep throw up rocks as they sped to the infirmary. By that time he was saying a coherent prayer for the brakeman, but he was interrupted by the yardmaster, an H&S Company staff sergeant, asking, "What happened, Don? Did you see anything? Hear anything?"

Don was slow to reply. He took a deep breath and told the sergeant, "Nick was walking between Tracks 14 and 15 toward a skewed joint near the departure lead. He stepped left to avoid a busted drawbar that was there between the tracks, and I guess he didn't hear the cut rolling down on him. I yelled, but I guess he was too far away. They were switching somewhere over there around Track 18, so it was loud down there.

"He got hit by the lead car. It looked like the pin-puller got him. And then he disappeared from sight. He—" Then Don drifted off. The young brakeman started to weave back and forth on his feet, his eyes rolled up in their sockets, his knees buckled, and he passed out. He was lucky the sergeant knew what to watch for—he'd seen the symptoms before. He caught the young brakeman before he hit the ballast.

Nick Costello would survive the injury, without his left leg. And while the accident changed his life in unimaginable ways, the cold predictability of what had happened to him was as certain as betting on the sunrise. Railroading chews men up.

Nick was the second major casualty for the battalion. Considering the conditions under which the 721st operated, their safety record was amazingly good. They were busy and they were overworked. There had been plenty of lesser injuries—twists, cuts, sprains, bruises, and even some broken bones—injuries that would heal. Nevertheless production was moving right along.

25

Stepping Up

Back in June, when the 721st was still recovering from the fire and the rainstorms, everything was difficult. Frantically trying to reconstruct records, they had to make four requests to get typewriters from Calcutta. Then they couldn't get the proper forms to retype the paperwork. The men were eating out of a field mess set up in the middle of a rice paddy as the monsoon bore down upon them. To say their situation was bleak was to put an unwarranted positive twist on things.

Company B was living in boxcars near the locomotive shed and trying its best to direct the uneducated and unmotivated Indian wallahs. The men often had to do precision work in service pits that were flooded with muddy, oily sludge. Still the company recorded only a single engine failure during these trying times.

In July the rains got worse. The men went to work in rubber boots, and most of the tracks disappeared underwater. There were many derailments and accidents because of ballast washouts. Overhead, signals shorted and wires fell. Repairs were made by overworked linemen who climbed the slick wet poles to set things right.

The men of H&S Company Signal Section had worked hard to improve the communications at Parbatipur. Now they were trying to save what they had accomplished. Upon arrival the signalmen had replaced the outdated Indian network with twisted-pair lines that ran from camp to town and from Parbatipur Yards to all the yardmaster offices. They had also brought in a telephone exchange switchboard and replaced the beaten-up Indian phones with new U.S. models. Their work, like that of the other companies, was arduous, dangerous, and frustrating. But as unlikely as it might seem, progress was being made.

Transshipment from broad gauge to metre gauge increased in

June, and the battalion reached 77 percent of its target tonnage. The main bottleneck, a problem that would plague their operation for months, was a lack of metre-gauge empties (unloaded rolling stock). Still they made do, often working without the heavy-lift steam crane that was prone to breakdowns and hard to supply with repair parts. Much of the time transshipment crews had to use the lighter gasoline cranes and improvise ways of getting the job done. They also trained the Indian crews on the proper use of the equipment—always a challenging proposition.

Looking to the future, the battalion began redesigning the yards and altering tracks. High on their list of improvements were new petroleum and fuel lines and new transshipment sheds. But these projects moved slowly because they were dependent upon the Indian workforce for construction labor. The biggest project, a new North Yard, seemed only a dream even though it was scheduled for completion by the end of the year.

July saw some progress in reconstruction of the battalion's camp. During the last week of the month the Battalion Headquarters and Post Exchange were moved to the new location. But no sooner had they set up shop than the rains nearly washed away the new buildings. Quickly the battalion built a drainage ditch to direct the deluge a quarter mile away from camp toward lower ground to the southwest. Late in the month a new indoor mess hall was opened with much applause from hungry GIs.

But the new camp construction suffered from a problem: the ground it was built on was man-made fill to elevate it above the local water table. The fresh fill hadn't settled before construction began, so the concrete floors sank. Some buildings had to be refloored three times before the sinking stopped, and every time they repoured the floors they had to reinforce the buildings' frames.

August arrived and the rains still came. But at last Company B began moving from their boxcars into new tents in the camp area proper. This was a godsend for their morale. Although the move wouldn't be complete until September, just the idea that better times were coming lifted their spirits. Their improved living conditions helped fortify the men for the work that lay ahead.

That month the battalion handled 59,369 cars, an increase of 1,995 over the previous month. They operated 930 trains, and, although that was a decrease of 27 over the previous month, the average length of each train increased by more than 4 cars, bringing the average train length to 66 cars. The transshipment operation increased as well and reached 81 percent of its target tonnage. Lack of empty metre-gauge cars created most of the transshipment backlog, and without the proper lift equipment most of the heavy loads were sent to Santahar to be worked.

Warehousing also improved during the month. And that was a good thing because the 721st had become the de facto quartermasters for the entire area. The battalion found itself supplying the 758th Shop Battalion detachment at Saidpur and other nearby units, among them the pipeliners and covert SACO and OSS operations. SACO, the Sino-American Cooperative Organization, was a U.S. Naval Group operating behind Japanese lines in China, much like the OSS. SACO ran a classified installation just outside of Jorhat where they stockpiled supplies and dispatched their operatives.

September saw the return of drier, temperate weather, and with the improving weather spirits picked up as well. H&S Company installed a public address system for the camp and aired daily programs. The battalion opened a day room were the men could read and relax and play Ping-Pong; it was stocked with newspapers, magazines, and books and was nicely furnished. With the fall of Myitkyina, the battalion was ordered to send more men to operate the local railway, now clear of Japanese.

September also saw a sharp rise in personnel transshipment with heavy through-movement to Katihar. These eastbound troop carriers were filled with the leading edge of the half-million Allied soldiers that would retake Burma and, as the plan called for, move on to China for the eventual invasion of Japan. Because of the heavy personnel traffic, some of the freight tonnage suffered. That month transshipment slipped to 73 percent of target and the car count dropped by 13 percent. The month also saw the introduction of refrigerator cars built at the Saidpur shops to move fresh meat from Parbatipur to Ledo. Something else took to the rails as well:

a new number called the Red Cross Trainmobile. The Parbatipur-based Trainmobile, one of two used during the war, with the other operating in the Persian Gulf area, brought entertainment and refreshments to remote outposts in Burma and India. It consisted of an engine and tender, a freight car with cooking and refrigeration equipment, and a caboose that served as living quarters for three Red Cross women who traveled onboard.[1] Always a welcome sight, the Trainmobile brought games, athletic equipment, stationery, cards, and other items of comfort to GIs and Allied soldiers far from home. On its maiden trip its crew handed out 30,000 donuts over thirty days.[2]

There were three derailments on the main line during the month that caused its blockage for a total of over twenty-two hours. One blockage of over seven hours was due to a fire that began when the Calcutta-to-China pipeline that paralleled the railroad main line failed. The leaking gasoline ignited and set ablaze all of the signal poles and communications equipment along 350 feet of track. The only silver lining in this disaster was that the new equipment used to make repairs allowed the battalion to activate a teletype system to speed communications.

The inauguration of a GI-staffed school for Indian workers took place in September. Indian Pioneers—units of the colonial army—as well as civilian laborers were taught the basics of stevedoring, operation of cranes and loading equipment, and the general system behind U.S. commercial shipping. The 721st got assistance in this enterprise from the port battalions working out of Calcutta and by the end of the month had set up a well-equipped classroom and training area in Parbatipur.

October was a drier month still, and work around the yards and camp started to shape up in earnest. Traffic hit 49,867 cars with 811 trains operated for an average of 61 cars per train. But these numbers were hard to compare to earlier figures because the car-counting formula was changed on orders from the 705th Railway Grand Division.

Obtaining railroad supplies remained a niggling problem. The men simply couldn't count on having what they needed to get the job done. One item, definitely not high-tech but nevertheless hard to come by, was shipping blocks. These wedge-shaped pieces of wood were used to chock equipment and supplies to rolling stock and keep everything moving in the same direction. As many as 30,000 blocks per week were used at Parbatipur. When the Railway Stores Department couldn't provide the blocks, the battalion begun cutting trees all along the railroad's right-of-way, eventually clearing miles of property just to get the wood they needed. The 721st also needed nearly twenty tons of wire and cable every month just to secure loads—not to mention the wire they needed to tether their rented mongooses to their tents at night. (The GIs rented mongooses from Indian natives and tethered them to their tents at night to discourage the snakes. They used wire to harness them so the wily critters wouldn't chew through their leashes.) By year's end the demand for wedges and wire had reached new peaks. In December the battalion used 100,000 wedges, 14,000 five-foot-long 4x4 stakes, and 130 tons of wire. To procure the necessary materials the battalion essentially cleared every tree in sight and started stripping the fences from around the railroad property for their wire.

During November the traffic increased substantially, with the battalion handling 58,060 cars in 1,003 trains. A record for transshipment was set on November 15, when 609 metre-gauge cars were loaded from 353 broad-gauge cars in one day. The battalion loaded a total of 13,873 metre-gauge cars that month, an increase of 403 cars over the previous month. Military stores transshipment in November reached 194 percent of target, and to speed train movement new double track was opened between Rangpur and Bhutsara.

November also brought more work for Company B. They received the job of converting over 1,000 War Department flat cars to gondolas, cars with open tops and steel sides. The "gons," as they were called, were needed to expedite the handling of heavy-lift shipments. The men devised a production line that, when supplies were available, could turn out a finished gondola, stenciled and painted, in just over thirty minutes. And as if Company B's dance card wasn't full enough, the Grand Division decided it would be a good idea to vacuum-equip all War Department cars and assigned most of the work to the 721st, which meant the work went to the already very busy men of Company B. They took it all in stride and turned out over 100 modified cars per month.

While November saw the agony of Nick Costello's accident, not all the news was gloomy. The weather continued to improve, with daytime temperatures remaining cool and the nights chilly. There was also an increase in USO stage shows.

The main line was blocked a total of thirty-four hours in November because of two pipeline leaks and three derailments. The worst wreck happened between Shampur and Barabari; the damage was so extensive and so many cars had derailed that the battalion had to build an emergency track around the wreck.

Traffic improved in December; the battalion handled 67,660 cars in 1,160 trains, an impressive increase of 9,600 cars over the month of November. Total metre-gauge equipment transshipped during the month came to 16,394, an increase of 2,521 cars.

Construction of new railroad was finally shaping up as the year drew to a close. The main line was opened from Badarganj through Bauchandi to Shampur, and from Rangpur to Tista Bridge. These improvements meant double-track movement was now possible over these sections, which allowed for higher track speeds. In December the average eastbound freight moved at 11 miles per hour and the average westbound increased that by 2.2 miles per hour, thanks to fewer work trains for the freight and passenger service to negotiate around.[3]

The men were motivated, the war was going well, and the freight was moving. To some the war was a grand adventure. To others it was a living hell. Most were somewhere between the extremes. Taken as a whole the 721st was dealing with their war very well. Most important, the freight kept going through.

26

Another Christmas

The radio was set up at the far end of the mess hall and the sound came though the public address speakers. The GIs were smoking, talking, sitting on tabletops or backward in their chairs. They couldn't get enough of the familiar routines and comforting banter. Their laughter was the sound of soulful relief.

The hall was decorated with imitation Christmas trees of cardboard since the battalion had cut all the trees in the area for blocking freight loads. Red and green crepe paper hung from the ceiling, and along its twisted length were pinned greeting cards and paper ornaments. The men had enjoyed a wonderful American-style meal on Christmas Day, and as they sat listening to the broadcast they enjoyed its leftovers. Some still had their Red Cross food packages; many snacked on baked goods sent from home. Everybody shared.

The Christmas meal had been heart-warming. Although it would never be as scrumptious, cozy, and personal as being back in the States at a family dinner, the men greatly appreciated the often berated cooking crew's efforts—especially after their disappointing Thanksgiving. A little more than a month earlier the battalion had pulled out all the stops and called in many considerable favors but still couldn't come up with fresh turkeys from Darjeeling, the only place in India they seemed to be available.

Now everybody was in a good mood, even though they were celebrating a day late with a recorded broadcast on Armed Forces Radio. Jim Hantzis and Nels Whittaker sat on a long bench with their feet stretched out in front of them and their backs against the wall.

Danny Kaye had just finished his number from *Up in Arms* when the old master W. C. Fields was introduced. His would be a monologue; he liked to work alone: "Throughout the Middle Ages the use of liquor was universal. Drunkenness was so common, it was unnoticed. They called it the Middle Ages because no one was able to walk home . . . unless they were between two other fellows. [Laughter.] I was the middle guy." Fields went on for ten minutes, then finished with his antidote for a hangover.

Judy Garland took the stage and sang "The Trolley Song." Then Spencer Tracy told the story of Pablo and the small donkey. For the big wrap-up of the two-hour show Dinah Shore sang "O Little Town of Bethlehem," Garland sang "O Come All Ye Faithful," Ginny Simms sang "The First Noel," Virginia O'Brien did "God Rest Ye Merry, Gentlemen," Dorothy Lamour styled "Deck the Halls," and Frances Langford sang "It Came Upon the Midnight Clear." Most of the men in the mess hall joined in on "Silent Night," some with tears in their eyes. The ones who didn't sing sat in deep reflection.

27

Milepost 103

The overloaded Jimmy rattled to beat the band as it lurked left and right in the hardened ruts. George's well-muscled arms swung the big steering wheel back and forth as if he were twisting off dance moves at the Reno Club in Kansas City on a Saturday night. The powerful engine's rhythmic rumble filled the metal cab with a cadence so loud that George had to shout to make his point. But he didn't mind; he was mad anyway. You'd think the truck was traveling 100 miles an hour, but the two men had been trudging along in low range, pulling stumps for over an hour, negotiating a rough section of steep roadway.

"It's a crying damn shame!" George yelled into the truck's windshield, never taking his eyes off the road ahead. "That's all I can say. We lug our butts halfway around the world, stick out our necks for these people, and they don't want us in their country because we're colored! I say they can go to hell. Let's ship all these supplies back to the States and let them fight it out on their own."

Bernie nodded.

"Hell, Chinese drivers," George continued. "Most of these guys couldn't handle anything bigger than a rickshaw. Wait till they hit a washout at five thousand feet rolling down Pangsau Pass through those switchbacks into the Hakawng Valley. Or start working those twenty-one horseshoes between Chen-Yi and Kweiyang or come heading down Chinglo Hill in a deuce-and-a-half loaded to the gills with ammunition and explosives. Then we'll all see just how good they are. Then they can turn around and do it all over again in the dark while it's raining. I just think it's a crying shame."

And Bernie, a reserved man by nature, nodded some more.

"At least they could double us up in a truck, you know, one of us guys and one Chinese guy. At least that way it would look good, you know, make some good pictures for back in the States. It burns my ass."

Bernie, an accidental audience of one, had only just begun to get his earful of George's nonstop rant. The motivation for George's tirade was the order that had just come down regarding drivers for the first official army convoy into Kunming. All Bernie could do was nod his head, which he was doing anyway thanks to the rutted roads they were driving.

Then Bernie saw a road sign that caught his attention. It was one of dozens of improvised warnings that dotted the berm of the Ledo Road, placed there by construction crews with too much time on their hands. This one had a shapely African American girl in a short skirt and high heels on the left side, tastefully drawn with practiced attention to detail, and on the right side these lines:

> Listen cats, I ain't jivin'
> Take it easy while you're drivin'
> —Speed Limit 25 m.p.h.—

In hopes of distracting George from his rant, Bernie asked, "You see that?"

George replied, "Yeah, she's lookin' good, but who they foolin'? You couldn't do twenty-five on this road if you had to." Then, without missing a beat, he went right back to his editorial: "Hell, I'd like to see one of those Chinese drivers get it up to twenty-five comin' down through here! Boy, I bet . . ."

And Bernie nodded again.

George was right. The Chinese drivers wouldn't be able to handle it. When the time came to turn over the task of driving the road, the results were frightening. In the first Chinese-manned convoy, in early February 1945, of the ninety trucks that left Ledo only sixty-six reached Pangsau Pass, less than thirty-eight miles away—thirty-eight easy miles at that.[1] And they still had a thousand miles to go. Even with intense training the problem persisted. The Chinese recruits were just too raw and sickly for the job. The U.S. Army finally gave up and hired Indian drivers.

But even the Indians, although better fit for the job, were not immune to the road's hardships. And that went for the American quartermaster truckers as well. The standard time for a one-way trip from Ledo to Kunming was supposed to be ten days, but it was common for the ordeal to last twelve to fifteen. Wrecks, of course, were always a problem. Driving over a cliff was indeed a health hazard. But it took no time at all for medical officers to report that drivers of all nationalities suffered from increased cases of dust pneumonia, cysts, fatigue, and kidney ailments from the rough and dirty ride.[2]

The order that bothered George so much had come down that morning. It specified that only Chinese drivers would be used on the final leg of their dangerous trip, when the convoy entered Kunming, because, according to Chiang Kai-shek, a "critical situation" might arise over the use of African American drivers in China, whom the western Chinese had never before seen.

Of course Bernie and George couldn't have known halfway along their route that Chiang would eventually relent and allow African American drivers as far as Kunming—but only that far and no farther east.[3] Nevertheless the first convoy—the one for the history books—would have Chinese drivers first in line, which was just plain galling to Bernie, George, the rest of the black drivers, and most of the other GIs as well. There were about 15,000 U.S. troops in India, Burma, and China building and working the Ledo Road, and roughly 60 percent were African Americans.[4]

On January 12, 1945, with the aid of white-gloved military police, 113 vehicles formed at Ledo. These vehicles were to be the first convoy to drive the entire distance of the Ledo Road, 1,079 miles, all the way to Kunming. These men would be the first to finally bust the land blockade of China imposed by Japan when Burma fell in early 1942. The road wasn't exactly complete, and it wasn't exactly secure, but they rolled out anyway.

Brig. Gen. Lewis Andrew Pick was in the lead Jeep, and rightfully so. He was the proud father of the road that many detractors swore couldn't be built. The Ledo Road, or as the GIs called it, "Pick's Pike," would go down as one of history's most impressive wartime engineering accomplishments. Pick had done the impossible in a little more than two years for roughly $150 million.

The total cost, however, had to be measured in lives as well. Only forty-two miles had been constructed through friendly territory; the rest had been taken yard by yard from the Japanese.[5] Besides the 624 GIs who had died in combat, 63 died of typhus, 11 of malaria, 53 drowned, 44 died in road accidents, and 173 perished in aircraft accidents. Another 165 men lost their lives to miscellaneous accidents and illnesses. All told, 1,133 men died during the road's construction, making the human cost roughly a man a mile.[6]

Each army engineer unit that had worked on the road got the privilege of designating a driver for the first convoy. They drove heavy cargo trucks, mostly two-and-a-half-ton, six-wheel-drive GMCs, called Jimmies, with duel tires on the four rear hubs. Mixed in with the big rigs were weapons carriers, Jeeps, and ambulances. Some of the trucks pulled artillery. The convoy also picked up motorcycle escorts at ceremonial points along the way. The Jimmies hauled supplies of all sorts, from ammo to K-rations, and on the passenger manifest were sixty-five radio, magazine, and newspaper correspondents, two of them African American.[7] Some of the GIs noted with concerned irony that there were more correspondents aboard than guards.

After a brief send-off from General Sultan, a lot of celebratory signage, and a barrage of photo flashes, General Pick gave the order to move out, and the six-mile-long mechanical snake began to wind its way into the Naga Hills. The GIs waved as their trucks lurched forward and shouted "Ding hao!" to their Chinese counterparts. The locals—Indian laborers, barefoot Nagas in gay costumes, and Kachin tribesmen—lined the road cheering and waving.

At milepost 34.5 the convoy reached Hell Gate and began its assent of Pangsau Pass, approaching the border with Burma. At the summit they stopped to view the white tips of the Himalayas in the northern distance stretching like stone stairs to heaven. Then the drivers stared into the deadly abyss lying far below, just beyond their running boards. There were no guardrails on the Ledo Road, and their journey had just begun.

At night they slept in jungle hammocks strung between vehicles when no other shelter was available. They ate ten-to-one field rations with delightful offerings of uncooked bacon, premixed cereal, and English stew. After baking in the humidity and heat of the lowlands they bathed in the cool streams that never seemed far away. At the other extreme, when the convoy stopped at the higher altitudes, nighttime brought chilly air and the drivers developed a great fondness for wool blankets or any covering to keep them warm.

On January 15 the convoy reached Myitkyina and came to a halt. Ahead the Japanese had the road under fire past Namhkam. The job of clearing the Japanese belonged to the Chinese 112th and 113th Regiments of the Thirty-eighth Division, two of Stilwell's old units. The 113th moved along the roadway and the 112th paralleled them through the hills.

By January 23 they had engaged retreating Japanese and killed at least sixty-seven,[8] and somewhere in the hills there was still a 150mm howitzer raining shells onto the road. After its position was uncovered and reported by an observation plane the Chinese began to pound it with their artillery and the enemy gun fell silent.

Meanwhile the convoy waited. The drivers cleaned up in a special bivouac area in the center of town, got some chow, and took in a Hedy Lamarr movie. Of course waiting is not the newsworthy event correspondents crave; press briefings were humorous at first but soon became a bit tense. You see, Pick's convoy wasn't the only game in town.

28

The Road Less Traveled

In August, after the Marauders had finally secured Myitkyina, a mixed brigade of Chinese and fresh Americans was designated the Mars Task Force and replaced the spent jungle fighters. Upon its activation the Mars Task Force sent a patrol on a nine-day exploratory march to find a cutoff to China in case the Japanese couldn't be removed from the Ledo and Burma Roads.

They found one. It ran up and over the spine of the Himalayas to Tengchung, China. The highest passage came at 8,500 feet amid shear rock cliffs looming above the Burmese jungle.[1] Col. Robert Seedlock, whose American engineers worked out of Kunming, and C. C. Kung, the director of the Chinese Yunnan-Burma Highway Engineering Administration, were handed the responsibility of taming the "Tengchung serpent," turning the rugged mule path into a tractable motor road. And this, by the time Pick's convoy arrived in Myitkyina, they had accomplished—or nearly so.

Tired of waiting and perhaps hoping to grab some headlines, Seedlock ordered Lt. Hugh Pock to take three vehicles, an eleven-ton wrecker and two beat-up 6x6s, and head to Kunming using the cutoff, which the young officer did on January 20. This set the press corps buzzing. General Sultan reacted by putting a clamp on media coverage of the unofficial, abbreviated convoy. Poor Seedlock couldn't even get his picture taken with his departing bedraggled threesome.

It was a different story, however, once the Seedlock-Kung convoy reached Kunming on January 24. There the daring detail recounted a hair-raising story of how they salvaged a truck whose axle had fallen over a cliff and had to bulldoze an improvised path. The newshounds loved it, giving them a warm welcome and good coverage, after which the men also received laudatory greetings from

Prime Minister Winston Churchill, Field Marshall Bernard Law Montgomery, and Gen. Albert C. Wedemeyer.

But if it was headlines they sought, they were trumped by news out of Europe. The world, it seems, was more interested in the Soviet Union's capture of Warsaw and its quickening advance on Berlin. The public attention was also riveted on the U.S. and British efforts to contain Hitler's counteroffensive in the Battle of the Bulge.[2]

Now, to further instigate trouble, add to the confusion, and stir up the press, it must be reported that it was actually the U.S. Navy that first traveled the Ledo Road to Kunming. And they did it in an open Jeep—one Jeep—that bounded the full length of the road solo carrying two brave and brash souls. Lt. Conrad Bradshaw and sailor William White reached Ledo on January 12, with Pick and his convoy. But instead of getting in line they drove past the send-off ceremonies, the assembled dignitaries, and the white-gloved MPs and kept right on going—for 1,079 miles.

Bradshaw had decided that instead of doing his assigned job he should carry the SACO flag to Kunming and get there before the army. Technically he left his Jorhat assignment without orders, which made him AWOL, absent without leave. He and White arrived in Kunming without a scratch four days ahead of General Pick, driving right through the Japanese shelling that had held up the convoy. Of course SACO could never *officially* sanction such blatant nose-thumbing at the army, so they reprimanded their errant officer fittingly: Bradshaw was ordered to file a report about his trip.[3]

Irritated by the grandstanding, General Pick still had 110 vehicles to get safely to Kunming. So, on the morning of January 23, after an eight-day delay, he lifted his trademark pilgrim's stick into the foggy morning air and pointed toward China. It's not clear that the theatrical general fully grasped the spiritual significance of the wooden staff he held aloft for the cameras. In Burmese Buddhist culture a pilgrim's stick symbolized man's *humble* role in the order of nature. Regardless, the unbowed tamer of nature was off.

But even if nature had allowed him and his convoy to pass

unfazed—which it didn't—the Japanese had other plans. And the stick the Allies waved at them was the Chinese Thirty-eighth Division.

On the same day Pick restarted his convoy, the Japanese decided to withdraw their Fifty-sixth Division from the Ledo Road area as part of their new strategy for holding southern Burma. The Chinese Thirty-eighth Division, however, thought the Japanese were still in the neighborhood and consequently were on full alert. What they didn't know or what someone hadn't communicated very well was that their own countrymen, troops of the China-based Y Force, had been working the Japanese problem from the other side of the border.

On January 27 the Chinese Thirty-eighth Division in Burma launched an attack into the area where they believed the Japanese to be and ran instead into the blue-uniformed Y Force advancing from China. The good news is that the commanders were able to call off a planned artillery bombardment of Y Force's position. But some tanks with the Thirty-eighth Division didn't get the word and opened fire. Soon small arms fire was flying in both directions. Once again the Chinese were shooting their own, just as at Myitkyina. The burning fuse on this explosive situation was bravely snuffed by Brig. Gen. George Sliney, who walked between the two units yelling, "Cease fire!" With this act of stony courage he unintentionally became the first of Pick's convoy to cross the Burma-China border, thus ending the Japanese blockade.

On the morning of the January 28 the convoy once again rolled out. Upon leaving Mu-se after a two-hour ceremony the drivers breathed easier when they left the dirt and gravel path of the Ledo Road, the road they had been traveling, and linked up with the macadam highway of the Burma Road. A few hours later, upon their official crossing of the border and arrival in war-torn Wanting, China, they were greeted by an impressive assemblage of dignitaries. General Sultan and Gen. Claire Chennault were there, as were Gen. Howard C. Davidson, head of the Tenth Air Force, Maj. Gen. Francis W. Festing of the British Thirty-sixth Division, Gen. Sun Li-jen with the Thirty-eighth Division, Gen. Wei Li-huang of Y Force, and Dr. T. V. Soong, the foreign minister of China. Back in the States General Stilwell radioed his best wishes and told all, "I take my hat off to the men who fought for [the Ledo Road] and built it."[4] As they rumbled out of town the procession drove past a hand-painted sign that read:

> The first convoy over the "Ledo Road" passed this point at 2:00 p.m. on 28th January, 1945 thus establishing a land link with China from India.
>
> The capture of Lashio by the Japanese had severed China from land communications with the outside world since May 1942. With the opening of this road, America is implementing her promise made to China in the dark days of retreat, to give our allies the means of Victory.

The driving was relatively smooth for the next week. The convoy was in Chinese-controlled territory now, and the road was well maintained. The lush green countryside of Burma gave way to the often desolate red and gray hills of Yunnan. The convoy first transited the Mekong River, snaking down its gorge and up the other side, but the Mekong was just a preview of coming attractions. The last big thrill was negotiating the Salween River Gorge, where Maj. John Ausland, an old China hand who had traveled extensively in Yunnan Province, compared the crossing to "going down the Grand Canyon and up the other side."[5] Drivers first descended 2,000 feet through thirty-five staple-curve turns, crossed a suspension bridge high above the raging river, then climbed out of the chasm in low gear, all the while praying not to add their rig to the wreck-littered junkyard far below.

On the night of February 3 the convoy slept at Lake Tien Chih, just outside of Kunming. They were high in the mountains and it was cold. The next morning the Chinese drivers took over the lead trucks, with George seething all the while and Bernie still nodding.

All 110 vehicles rolled into Kunming, with Pick in the lead Jeep standing and waving his stick as they crossed a yellow-ribbon finish line at the city's West Gate. Pick hadn't lost a single truck. At the ribbon the general was greeted by the provincial governor, Lung Yun, a Japanese confidant, who presented him with a silk banner imprinted with the Chinese characters for "The Road to Victory."[6] That evening Lung staged a banquet with Lily Pons, the Franco-American opera star, and her husband and conductor, Andre Kostelanetz.

The first convoy—the first official convoy—to break the Japanese blockade had arrived. The Ledo Road was a success and would soon begin delivering substantial tonnage over a 14,000-mile supply line running from the West Coast of the United States through India and Burma to Kunming, China. It was the longest line of communication ever maintained in war, and everybody did their part, especially America's soldier railroaders, to make it happen.

Old Chiang Kai-shek even had a change of heart and graciously suggested that the Ledo Road be renamed the Stilwell Road. Vinegar Joe, it can be assumed, was not overly thrilled.

. . .

On the day the convoy arrived in Kunming another convoy of sorts gathered in a town on the northern shore of the Black Sea, Yalta. This convoy was made up of political heavyweights, and their meeting in the Crimean city would be the final rendezvous of the Big Three: Franklin Roosevelt, Josef Stalin, and Winston Churchill.

The Soviet Army had reached the Oder River and was preparing for the final attack on Berlin. The day before the conference was to start, Stalin was so confident of his military position that he ordered his defense chief, Marshal Georgy Zhukov, to hold his forces in place while the week-long conference was in session.

Stalin's liberation of Poland was now complete. In July 1944 Russian troops had overrun the Nazis' extermination camps at Majdanek and then Belzec, Sobibor, and Treblinka. In January 1945, on the eve of Yalta, Soviet troops entered Auschwitz, the largest death camp in the Nazi system. There, besides the ovens and 7,650 starving prisoners, the Red Army found warehouses of personal belongings, hundreds of thousands of men's suits, more than 800,000 women's outfits, and more than 14,000 pounds of human hair.[7] So the Allies sitting at the conference table on the Crimea were well aware of the Nazi horror with which they were dealing. Come April the Americans would liberate Buchenwald and see for themselves.

Stalin, the Georgian son of a cobbler and a washerwoman, now commanded the largest army in Europe, with twelve million soldiers in 300 divisions. Roosevelt, a scion of a patrician New York family, had four million men in eighty-five divisions; his troops were still west of the Rhine and lucky that the Germans hadn't cut them in half at the Battle of the Bulge.

Strategic bombing had devastated German urban and industrial areas. Dresden, the last untouched major city, the country's seventh largest, would be destroyed the night of February 13, when Churchill, perhaps at Stalin's request, returned to England and ordered its bombing. That night, "Florence on the Elbe," as the capital of Saxony was known, would receive 796 Avro Lancaster heavy bombers and nine lighter de Havilland Mosquitoes courtesy of RAF Bomber Command. The planes attacked in two raids and dropped 1,478 tons of high explosive and 1,182 tons of incendiaries on the city.[8] The next day the Americans arrived with 527 aircraft and delivered 953 tons of high explosives and 294 tons of incendiary bombs.[9] After the first wave of British bombers a firestorm engulfed the city center and the railroad marshaling yards. This man-made hell on earth along with continued bombing by the British and Americans over the next two days killed between 35,000 and 135,000 people.[10]

When Roosevelt addressed Congress on March 1, 1945, to report on the Yalta Conference he did it seated. He was a weak man now. Members of Congress couldn't help but notice his pale complexion, uneven speech, and lifeless stare. In a month and a half he would be dead from a massive cerebral hemorrhage.

Roosevelt's speech dwelled heavily on the need to construct the political framework for world peace, at least as far as Europe was concerned. The Pacific was another story. Things there were a bit more up in the air than in Europe. Although it went unsaid in his address, Roosevelt had gained a promise from Stalin to declare war on Japan two to three months after Germany's surrender.

At Yalta, Stalin pretended to know nothing about the atomic

bomb. Roosevelt, after all, had yet to tell him. Churchill had known the secret since 1942, when he urged Roosevelt to aggressively undertake the Manhattan Project. Churchill envisioned an Anglo-American monopoly on atomic power to contain Stalin.[11]

Regardless of the Great Powers' political intrigue, there was no secret about what needed to be accomplished after Europe. The president summed up the work to be done in the Pacific this way:

> Quite naturally, this conference concerned itself only with the European war and with the political problems of Europe, and not with the Pacific war.
>
> In Malta, however, our combined British and American staffs made their plans to increase the attack against Japan.
>
> The Japanese warlords know that they are not being overlooked. They have felt the force of our B-29s, and our carrier planes. They have felt the naval might of the United States, and do not appear very anxious to come out and try it again.
>
> The Japs know what it means to hear that "The United States Marines have landed." And we can add, having Iwo Jima in mind, "that the situation is well in hand."
>
> They also know what is in store for the homeland of Japan now that General MacArthur has completed his magnificent march back to Manila, and that Admiral Nimitz is establishing his air bases right in their own back yard.
>
> But, lest somebody else lay off work in the United States, I can repeat what I have said, even in my sleep, a short sentence, "We haven't won the wars yet," with an "s" on wars.
>
> It is a long tough road to Tokyo. It is longer to go to Tokyo than it is to Berlin, in every sense of the word.
>
> The defeat of Germany will not mean the end of the war against Japan. On the contrary, we must be prepared for a long and costly struggle in the Pacific. But the unconditional surrender of Japan is as essential as the defeat of Germany. I say that advisedly, with the thought in mind that that is especially true if our plans for world peace are to succeed. For Japanese militarism must be wiped out as thoroughly as German militarism.[12]

Perhaps a bit measured and lacking in color for the average GI, but nevertheless a sobering summary of what lay ahead. At roughly the same time Roosevelt was speaking, another well-known authority on the war took a crack at describing what had to be done in CBI and the rest of the Pacific. General Stilwell, now in Washington, gave an interview to the Allied News Service and United Press. It appeared in the February 8, 1945, edition of *Roundup*, the GI newspaper in the CBI theater.

Long War in Pacific—Stilwell

NEW YORK (ANS-UP)—Gen. Joseph W. Stilwell, newly-appointed head of the Army Ground Forces, grimly stated this week that the war in the Pacific would not be won until long after Germany is defeated.

Speaking with his usual directness, the former CBI commander predicted the Japanese would soon be forced out of Burma, but warned they would continue to fight even after their home islands were conquered.

Stilwell forecast that the war would have to be fought out on the continent of Asia. He estimated that the Japanese are prepared to use 4,000,000 troops to defend their position on the Asiatic mainland. He said we have not even begun to cut into the Japanese reserves of manpower.

Touching on Burma, Stilwell stated the Allies may reach Rangoon in a few months, with a stiff resistance awaiting them. "Japan can be expected to hang on at Rangoon as long as possible," he said. He pointed out that when Rangoon is taken more supplies could be moved to China over the old Burma Road.

Stilwell praised the Chinese soldier but acknowledged that he had criticized the performance of high Chinese officers.

"I've been accused of complaining about the capability of higher commanders," he said. "I have done that, but I believe many of them were handicapped because they didn't have what we consider essential training in junior grades. When they've had experience and training they perform very effectively."

"Uncle Joe's" credo in the CBI was always that there was one way to win the war and that was "to kill Japs." He ended his press conference on the same note.

"There's an excess 1,000,000 births over deaths in Japan yearly," he pointed out. "At that rate you have to kill 10,000 of them weekly to keep even."

In the early months of 1945 the Ledo Road was ready, the Germans were doomed, and very few people knew of the atomic bomb—and those who did still didn't know if it would work.

The challenge of Japan remained. The GIs in India, Burma, and China were plugging away at the plan to make China logistically capable of handling a 500,000-man invasion taskforce that would jump off from Korea to the Japanese home islands on a date not yet specified. In early 1945 America's logistical and combat organizations were just starting to peak, and everyone was working around the clock to make them even better.

29

Toy Train to Shangri-La

Soon after the 721st Battalion arrived in Parbatipur the enlisted men were granted rotating leave—work allowing—ranging from a few days to two weeks. Of course the fire and the wind storm in March and April 1944 put a damper on men going anywhere, but as soon as the normal routine returned, leave rotation began again.

The GIs mostly visited Calcutta for the restaurants, especially Firpo's, where Jim Hantzis learned to love fried shrimp. Or they went to Renekhat for the rest camp, with its nearby Govind Ballabh Pant Sagar Lake, or Madras, with its long, inviting white sand Marina Beach.[1]

But the best relief from the weather, be it rain or heat, and the one closest at hand was to be found in Darjeeling, "Queen of the Hills," where the altitude and attitude were relaxing and refreshing. Following his visit in 1896, Mark Twain said of Darjeeling that it was "the one land that all men desire to see, and having seen once by even a glimpse would not give that glimpse for the shows of the rest of the world combined."[2] To the British and Americans, Darjeeling was exotic yet accessible, and more important, much of the year it was cool and dry. These two climatic advantages were the reason the British had decided to build a rest camp and convalescent center there a century earlier.

The first European explorers traipsed through this remote wonderland—a Shangri-La to their eyes—in February 1829. At that time the undeveloped, mud hut village that was to become Darjeeling was a part of the nation of Sikkim. This tiny country had the advantage, or disadvantage, of being surrounded on three sides by some of the tallest mountains on the planet, many summits rising above 23,000 feet. With Tibet and China to the northeast, Nepal to the west, and India on its southern border, the small country sat on highly valued crossroads property, and of course the British took note.

Topology might well be destiny. With two-thirds of its landmass snow-covered peaks, Sikkim's religious traditions—Animist, Hindu, and Buddhist—incorporated the belief that the gods lived in, and *were*, the mountains. At altitudes below 5,000 feet the flora offered an Eden-like composition of palms, bamboos, ferns, and orchids. At a little higher altitude, before the snowline, oak trees, laurel, maple, chestnut, magnolia, alder, birch, and rhododendron flourished. Sikkim was also the domain of pandas, goats, leopards, tigers, eagles, and cockatoos. The tiny land overflowed with mystical beliefs and hosted fantastic creatures, including bear gods, enchanted eagles, and what some called the Abominable Snowman, what the Nepalese called the Yeti, and what the locals called the Nee-Gued.

By 1835 the British had negotiated a deed for Darjeeling from the rajah of Sikkim to the East India Company. At the time the village consisted of about twenty earthen shelters on a hilltop and a native population of fewer than 100. In 1841 the British introduced a crop, pilfered from China, that would make Darjeeling world famous. Within twenty years tea cultivation grew into a multimillion-pound industry. In the immediate countryside surrounding Darjeeling a visitor could find forty gardens totaling 10,000 acres producing half a million pounds of the "Champagne of teas."

By the time America's soldier railroaders got a chance to visit, Darjeeling had a colorful population of around 50,000, with dozens of ethnic minorities and tribal groups. Hindi Gurkhas from eastern Nepal roamed its cobbled streets. Tibetan Buddhist lamas in flowing yellow robes shopped for vegetables alongside women whose striped brocade aprons sported handcrafted ornaments. Oriental Gurungs from western Nepal swatted the hindquarters of goats and cattle with willowy switches to keep them moving through the city. Short, fair-skinned aboriginal Mongolian Sikkims known as Lepchas, people of the ravines, peacefully walked the streets brushing past their more aggressive historical nemeses, the Dukpas from Bhutan, who were armed with their traditional long knives. All these people flowed into the hill town to escape the suffocating heat of India's malarial plains, practice their beliefs, and ply their wares.

To get there the men of the 721st took the Darjeeling Himalayan Railway, an oddity from the nineteenth century. With its tiny twenty-four-inch gauge track it was soon nicknamed "the Toy Train" by locals, a shorthand and gauge still used today. Its original fifty-one-mile route is a monument to innovative engineering in construction and locomotion.

The gradient of the railroad had to be held to a maximum of a foot rise for every twenty feet of track. Beyond this incline the engine would not have enough traction to pull or stop the weight of the train. The 7,000-foot ascent from Siliguri averaged 137 feet per mile and was made without tunnels. Engineers instead used a series of loops with names like Sensation Corner and Agony Point, as well as Z-crossings or switchbacks. In a Z-crossing the engine pulls up the first leg of the Z, then a brakeman throws a switch and the little locomotive pushes the train up the middle section; at the end of that section it stops for another switch, then continues to pull until the next switchback.

With over 900 bends in its route the travel speed was slow, but the scenery was breathtaking. The little train hugged the mountainsides along precipices where only mountain goats felt at home. For eight and a half hours a traveler was treated to dense forests, white orchids, cascading waterfalls, tea gardens, and flaming wildflowers—all the beauty the eye can take in and none of the speed to blur the wonder.

The railroad actually reached its apex before arriving at Darjeeling. At Ghoom, on the Indian-Nepal border, in front of a Tibetan Buddhist monastery the elevation topped out at 7,407 feet above sea level, the highest station in the world servicing a wheels-on-rails, non-cog railroad. (Cog railways gain traction by rack-and-pinion gearing.) The final four miles to Darjeeling were actually downhill and provided the GIs and other travelers with a storybook view of a magical city shrouded in mist set against mighty Kanchenjunga, the world's third highest mountain at 28,169 feet.

By the time the 721st discovered the little railroad it was handling over 260,000 passengers a year and 65,000 tons of freight. The typical train consist was a twenty-eight-ton Garrett eight-wheel, articulated engine and tender, first introduced in 1909 and still in use today, four passenger cars, and one van. The engine and tender, hinged in the middle, were a 0-4-0+0-4-0 wheel configuration. Thanks to the unit's ability to flex, it could operate around the frequent sharp turns.

To its GI passengers it was an odd sight indeed. Hantzis could reach the engine's handrail while standing on the ground; the little train would never be mistaken for a high-balling streamliner, but it got the job done nevertheless.[3] The GIs were amused by it but all the same respected its practicality. Most of all they wanted to visit Darjeeling, and the Toy Train was their ticket up the mountain.

When they came back down, the war was still on.

30

Crossing Irrawaddy

Help thy brother's boat across, and lo! thine own has reached the shore.

—Hindu proverb

"It's like trying to keep a bloody mare on a rein during mating season, this randy tub is," the young private muttered to his comrade as they stumbled along the muddy river bottom in the raging current. The struggling soldier was waist-deep trying to keep his balance and all his weight on the stern line.

"Bloody well right, mate. And you'd be a sight more lucky back in Blighty trying. If we 'adn't shed two stones marching the devil's hell of Burma, we might have the heft to tame this bugger," returned his buddy, a lanky unshaved lance corporal. He shared the private's predicament but was even more unfortunate to be charged with the boat's bow line.

The two frustrated fusiliers were dangerously deep in the swift current trying to steady the Goatley, and they had their hands full. The light collapsible canvas boat bucked their weight and unrelentingly pulled them downstream. They were living a dilemma: the deeper the boat pulled them into the muddy water, the more buoyant their bodies became and the less control they exerted. Their struggle was an Archimedean wager, a bet that the raging Irrawaddy, fueled by Burma's great hills to the north, was sure to win.

While the Goatley and its human anchors drifted, the captain of the boat, a royal engineer, struggled with a rope starter atop its small outboard motor. The burly middle-aged man yanked at the crankshaft pulley and cursed the stubborn engine under his breath in a salty Glaswegian dialect. The entire river bank smelled of oily petrol as the flooded motor first caught, then sputtered, but failed to fire. The rest of the platoon could only maintain cover and wait in the darkness. Those were their orders: wait—just like the rest of the battalion—and cross in turn.

Finally, following a particularly sharp string of verbal encouragement, the little engine coughed to life and let out a high-pitched ring-a-ding clamor. As the sapper carefully adjusted the carburetor's fuel tickler, he said to the young private at the boat's stern, "Get your men aboard, lad. Do it quickly."

The fusilier motioned the first platoon, and six of thirty soldiers climbed into the tipsy sixteen-foot craft, each gingerly handing off their No. 4 Mk I rifles crowned with short, pig-sticker bayonets. Into four other Goatleys waiting farther up the shoreline—boats whose engines had been more cooperative—scrambled the rest of the platoon. All told, theirs would be the third string of crossings that evening.

It was good to know that someone friendly to their cause was waiting on the other shore, but finding their comrades was going to be tough. Japanese snipers had extinguished the signal torch that marked the landing area just after the second string of boats had returned to the northern bank.

The battalion's crossing, 800 men in all, had started soon after darkness; the trip across the half-mile of dangerous water took a little more than thirty minutes in each direction. Royal Engineers and a scouting party of Special Boat Service commandos had designated channels across the river with rubber buoys to help the vulnerable little boats avoid hazards and sandbars. But the buoys were hard to see in the pitch of the moonless night and the current was powerful. Earlier that day sappers had measured the river's speed at six knots. The good news was that the two previous crossings had gone pretty much by the book, so far as anybody yet to cross could tell. Now, as the little boats cast off, fusiliers in the bows and sterns of each craft lashed them together so they wouldn't be separated.

As the river's swells broke over the low freeboards of the Goatleys the soldiers still wearing tin helmets, the ones who had yet to trade them for the more popular bush hats, used them to bail the small crafts. For the most part, the water going out equaled that coming in—the first rule of safe boating. As some bailed, others used short wooden paddles to help along the small motors.

The first twenty minutes of the crossing went well. Only sporadically did the platoon hear the sound of bullets striking the water's surface around them. Then, an instant later, they heard dull muzzle cracks announcing the enemy's position on the far shore. *But it's only rifle fire*, they thought to themselves in a strangely comforting validation. It was a disquieting reversal of cause and effect, the bullet striking before the sound, but at least—each man rationalized silently—they were out of machine-gun range. It seemed as though the Japanese lacked a fix on their position, and that too was good news. Also encouraging was the fact that the mortar shells harmlessly erupting in gusher spouts far off their port side seemed random and without accurate plot.

The restless soldiers, like moviegoers at an outdoor theater, watched muzzle flashes along the shoreline to their port. The distant fighting was playing out high on the approaching embankment. This, they assumed, was their D Company comrades returning fire and suppressing the Japanese defenders. *That's encouraging*, thought the transients, again each man to himself. Then, in the blink of an eye, their positive take on things vanished.

One hundred yards off the enemy shore riders in the second boat heard a ripping noise like someone tearing a bed sheet. Then they heard a loud crack and pop as a half-submerged tree stump and its jagged roots tore through the boat's light canvas hull and snapped a wooden spar as though it were a toothpick. The Goatley immediately began taking on water faster than its passengers could bail, valiantly though they tried. Soon the waterlogged craft was pulling the rest of the string out of the channel, off their mark, away from their comrades and down the relentless river. When the sinking boat began pulling under the other two boats attached to it, there was only one thing left to do. The order was given to abandon ship and cut the doomed craft adrift. The fusiliers rushed to take off everything that would weigh them down. They flung their ammo belts, grenades, and other gear to the nearest boats, but their footing was poor and there was no time to aim.

About fifty yards from Japanese-held territory everyone who had started out in the second boat was in the water trying to grab anything that floated—paddles, ammo boxes, anything. Only three men found the gunnels of the other boats. One was lost shortly after he entered the water, and the sapper, the only man in the boat issued a life vest, swam to shore towing a young private. Another man, a strong swimmer, was caught in the current and swept downstream. He had been lucky enough to get his boots off before abandoning the Goatley and had the presence of mind to swim with the current and try to angle his way to the far shore. After what seemed like an eternity in the chilly water he heard thrashing ahead and a familiar braying sound—familiar but out of place. Ten yards farther he intercepted a pack of transport mules swimming across the river and grabbed the coarse hair of one mule's tail. The pack was being led by a Burmese boatman and a royal engineer, who discovered the exhausted fusilier from D Company when the stubborn animals decided to take an unscheduled rest on a shallow sandbar, dragging the young soldier up with them.

Once on the southern shore, the platoon, formerly thirty men but now seventeen, was scattered with no communications. On their right flank they traded fire with a sniper, and every couple of minutes a fusilier would force the Japanese to move with a short burst of a 9mm Sten machine carbine. Thirty feet above them the enemy rolled grenades down the steep river bank, guessing at the platoon's position. Far off on their left flank they could hear mortars, spring grenades, machine guns, and steady rifle fire. There, they assumed, was the main force. But reuniting with them would not be easy.

The platoon faced a steep but climbable embankment atop which thick elephant grass taller than a man blocked their advance and presented no readymade paths to follow. Trying to maneuver through the sharp blades would be painful, but the bigger problem would be the noise their movement would create. It would make them easy targets for the concealed enemy. The platoon's prospects were bleak and their options few.

They got a big break when a brassy lance corporal accompanied by two fusiliers reached the berm of the embankment and established a position for the platoon's 7.7mm Bren submachine gun. The lance corporal stood on a rifle held like a step by the two fusiliers, the three of them looking like a tipsy acrobatic troupe. After hoisting the twenty-three-pound Bren and shoving it over the ledge, he righted the gun and, leaning into the steep bank for support, smacked the top of its barrel with his clenched fist, forcing the spiked tips of its bipod into the clay soil. He let the Bren sweep the terrain at the rate of 500 rounds a minute, 180 degrees in front of it and about one foot off the ground. The Bren mowed an arc of the elephant grass as if it were someone's front yard; as a result the grenades stopped rolling, the sniper fell silent, and the platoon scrambled up the ledge. At the top they dug in as best they could to spend the night.

The air was cold and the men were wet, some soaked to the bone during their crossing. Many had discarded their weapons and ammo to save their lives. Now the only sensible course was to wait until morning, when they could scout the area and try to regroup with the rest of D Company. For the next six hours that's what they did, teeth chattering all the while.

When morning broke, a scouting party moved upriver 700 yards to the east and found the company commander. There the bulk of D Company had concentrated and secured some high ground and a beachhead. Now they were busily setting up defensive positions and planning the next night's crossing for yet more units of the British Army Second Division. Their forced crossing accomplished, they were now forty-five miles north of Mandalay. The only thing between them, the city, and retaking Burma was the entire Japanese Area Army—about 100,000 men—fighting not for strategic advantage or battlefield position but for their lives. Everything was just as General Slim would have it.[1]

. . .

The victories at Kohima and Imphal brought General Slim around to Stilwell's way of thinking—that you win the war by killing Japanese. This proposition, as applied to Burma, meant that Slim had to destroy the Japanese Army and worry less about capturing cities.

The battle for India had been costly for both sides, but the Japanese suffered far the worse. Slim's timely estimation that Mutaguchi's gamble had cost him 65,000 men was spot-on, as confirmed after the war. Slim, who had seen much that was ugly and unpleasant, called the Japanese retreat from India "the ultimate beastliness of war."[2] As he pushed the Japanese east and south out of India and back into Burma, he looked upon the evidence strewn before him: the bloody carnage, the abandoned tanks, guns thrown aside, bodies leaned against trees, and streams damned with corpses. It convinced him that another mighty blow—quickly dealt—would destroy the off-balance enemy.

But Kimura, the new Japanese commander, was smart. He didn't conform to Slim's typecasting of a Japanese general officer—someone who was overbold, inflexible, and reluctant to change a plan once set in motion. Kimura was not the "military optimist" that Slim had so often enticed with a tantalizing but false opportunity, then entrapped and dispatched.[3] Kimura refused to fight where Slim first laid the bait, on the Shwebo Plain with the broad Irrawaddy River to protect the Japanese rear. Kimura had but twenty tanks to oppose Slim's mechanized armor on the open terrain, and the Japanese Air Force in Burma had been whittled down to only 64 overworked airplanes against 1,200 for the Allies.[4] The Japanese planes that hadn't been shot from the sky or bombed on the ground had been redeployed to the Philippines the previous October to stall the return of Gen. Douglas MacArthur.[5]

Instead Kimura ordered his retreating army to cross the Irrawaddy, oppose Slim's crossing, and then maneuver south and east, closer to Japanese supply lines. He planned to fight the British with the river as his first line of defense and turn its waters red with the blood of his enemy. West of the Irrawaddy Kimura left behind only suicide squads to harass and slow Slim's advancing army and ordered his Fifteenth Army to defend 250 miles of shoreline where the British would attempt to cross. But now behind his army, instead of a friendly river barrier, lay the rice of Burma's fertile delta and the oil at Yenangyaung, two commodities upon which the lives and fortunes of the Japanese depended.[6]

Kimura's decision not to fight on Shwebo disappointed Slim but did not dissuade him. As the ever-flexible Britisher worked the problem he fashioned maneuvers and supply lines that he readily admitted were on the margins of responsible leadership. His planning went beyond bold and bordered on reckless. He looked for unit commanders with "dash and spirit" who were "not too calculating of odds," men who understood that, above all else, the battle at hand was a race, run as always against the imminent monsoon.

Every time Slim thought he might be overestimating the ability of his men, he took the measure of their morale. Not once did he see the dodgy signs of weariness or contempt, only positive attitudes, new ideas, improvisation, and resourcefulness. He had been knighted only a month earlier, but he was nevertheless a soldier's general. He could see in his men's eyes that they were willing to march when ordered and where ordered, just as they had marched through the monsoon to pursue the retreating Japanese. He looked upon the platoons and companies, British, Indian, and Gurkha, and was inspired by the "high fighting value and hardihood of them all."[7]

With this reassurance he developed a double-ploy battle plan, one that required stealth, deception, precision, and discipline but would ultimately end the war in Burma. It was, by all accounts, one of the great military masterstrokes of World War II. As Slim and his staff made ready Operation Capital, however, there was a ghost in the room.

. . .

Back in March 1944, twelve days before his death, Orde Wingate had offered an inspired proposal to Mountbatten and Slim.[8] He had asked that his reserve Chindits be sent to Pakokku, then on to Meiktila, sixty-five miles to the east, to cut the Japanese main supply line and communications. Meiktila lay seventy-five miles south of Mandalay and 300 miles north of Rangoon and through it passed everything of importance to the enemy. It hosted supply dumps for the Japanese Fifteenth and Thirty-third armies, airfields, hospitals, and railroad links to Rangoon. At the time the proposal looked a bit like lunacy. But now, a year later, even though Slim would be "fighting with four and two-thirds British and Indian divisions, a river behind them and at the end of a precarious line of communication against five and a third Japanese divisions in their own selected positions," the odds, he thought, had turned in his favor.[9]

The attack on Meiktila, the scissors that would cut the Japanese Army in half, required that Kimura believe the real objective was Mandalay. To position his troops for the attack on Meiktila, Slim would need to secretly split his Fourteenth Army into two corps, move thousands of men and tanks 300 miles south into position on the far side of the Irrawaddy, and force a crossing for the main attack. It was a calculated gambit even with short and reliable supply lines. But short and reliable was not the case. The IV Corps, the all-important secret attack force upon whom the fate of the British Army in Burma might well depend, would be 400 miles from the Allies' railhead at Dimapur, and 250 miles of that distance was roadway that was passable only in fair weather.[10]

The Americans and Chinese, whose principal responsibility was to secure the north of Burma and the Ledo Road so supplies could flow uninterrupted to China, factored into Slim's plan as well. They formed the far northern component of the Fourteenth Army's left flank. Their presence required that Kimura detach some of his units to prevent an advance on Mandalay from the north. But, as always, the Chinese were complicating matters.

The Japanese were on the offensive in China. Their Operation Ichigo had succeeded in capturing a number of Allied airfields, and Chiang's army didn't look to be up to the challenge of fending them off. Predictably, with his arrogance firmly intact, Chiang *demanded* on February 23, 1945, the immediate return of *all* of his Chinese forces in Burma and that they should under no circumstances advance farther south than eighty miles northeast of Mandalay.[11] So General Sultan, commanding the combined forces in northern Burma, was ordered to transfer most of the Stilwell-trained Chinese to their homeland, along with their air support and some aircraft that had been supporting Slim's forces as well.

CROSSING IRRAWADDY

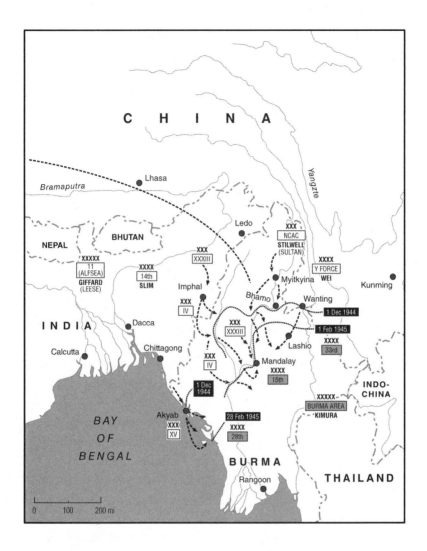

MAP 6. General Slim's campaign to retake Burma, November 1944–June
1945. NCAC is Northern Combat Area Command, also called X Force.
ALFSEA stands for Allied Land Forces South East Asia. X = 1 division. Corps
are designated with roman numerals (e.g., IV = IV Corps). Gen. Sir George
James Giffard was commander in chief of the Eleventh Army Group in India
and Burma. He was replaced by Gen. Oliver Leese in October 1944. Map by
Erin Greb.

This allowed the Japanese opposing the Allies in northern Burma to retire in good order to the south to fight against Slim at Mandalay.

For the time being the U.S. troops of the Mars Task Force stayed in Burma along with a healthy group of U.S. fighters and bombers. The Mars Task Force, the administrative offspring of Merrill's Marauders, was a premier fighting force with great mobility and high morale. But in mid-April they too were ordered to China. The few Chinese troops that remained in Burma advanced only as the Japanese retreated to Mandalay, and the security of the Ledo Road was placed in the hands of 2,500 tribesmen, mostly Kachin, under U.S. command. As the quicksand of Chinese-American politics shifted beneath his combat boots, Slim briefly noted his potential plight but just as quickly put the image from his mind. The Americans had promised him air support until he had taken Rangoon or June 1, whichever came first. Upon capturing Rangoon his army would be able to resupply from its coveted deepwater port. What he didn't want to imagine was the Fourteenth Army slogging its way toward Rangoon as the monsoon broke without air resupply. As the forward-looking Slim put it, "Sufficient for the day was the evil thereof!"[12]

Kimura was right: the indispensable first step was a forced crossing of the Irrawaddy, Burma's Rubicon. The great river, its name derived from the Sanskrit *Airavati*, "Elephant River," runs the length of the country, cutting it in half.[13] Starting as a trickle in the white glaciers of the high northern mountains, the river grew through 1,350 miles of Burma, flowing south to the Andaman Sea. The Japanese believed the river was "the line of change of the hearts of the Burmese people," a population whose allegiance they were quickly losing.[14] At the locations where General Slim's 65,000 troops would most likely force their crossing, it was often more than a mile wide. Slim's transit of the Irrawaddy would be the longest forced crossing attempted during World War II.

The logistics of getting across became a patchwork of improvised watercraft, flimsy canvas Goatleys, contracted Burmese boatmen, and worn-out landing craft brought over after use in the European theater. Slim had his engineers set up a boat yard factory to turn out wooden pontoons, barges, and gunboats. Some, like the animals—Slim's army moved on combined mechanical and animal transport—simply swam across.

One thing working to the advantage of the Allies was that the Japanese Fifteenth Army was stretched thin guarding 250 miles of shoreline. General Slim, a longtime practitioner of the art of exploiting Japanese weaknesses, knew the layout of their zones of defense. He knew that it was at the boundaries of these zones that they would be slow to respond because of their administrative inflexibilities. So it was at these points that many of the crossings were made.

The crossings started on January 14, 1945, when the 19th Division slipped into territory east of the Irrawaddy only forty miles north of Mandalay. By the end of the month the battle for the ancient city was under way. Over the next two months companies, battalions, regiments, and divisions poked holes in the Japanese lines along the Irrawaddy, established beachheads, and moved into position to attack the city. Slim's plan called for three thrusts: a feint from the north to draw away Japanese forces, followed by two purposeful advances from the south and southwest. But first they had to cross the river.

Every crossing was fraught with danger, even the lucky few that went unopposed. Each was determined by what were the best and safest locations to challenge the enemy and also for the picture it would present to Kimura. The illusion that Slim wanted the Japanese to believe was that he and his men were coming after Mandalay. That's why, on February 23, he sent the British Second Division across the river only ten miles from the city, a very well-defended area, while at the same time, 100 miles to the east, IV Corps secretly moved down the Gangaw Valley on hastily built roads, following close on the swinging tails of construction elephants to attack Meiktila.

The fictional location of Slim's force, the force actually advancing on Meiktila, was promoted by the establishment of a dummy corps headquarters through which all radio traffic was routed. That's why, as far as the high-level Japanese staff were aware—meeting by coincidence on February 26 at Meiktila—the quickly approaching British Nineteenth Division still resided somewhere near Sittaung on the far side of the Chindwin, sixty miles from Imphal. The smug Japanese staff officers dismissed reports from their local commanders that 2,000 vehicles were closing in on their position. They assumed it was a typographical error and simply erased a zero, then went about their business confidently believing that any attack on the important, well-defended town could be but a small raid.

Slim's vital thrust toward Meiktila with an armored column of the Seventeenth Division and the 255th Tank Brigade had crossed the Irrawaddy five days earlier. The swift force swept away the Japanese resistance. While the quality of the Japanese soldiers that Slim's commanders now encountered seemed to be slipping, there were still plenty of true believers to be dealt with. For instance, when the Durham Light Infantry fought to secure its bridgehead near Ngazun they were pitted against a thirty-five-man suicide unit, all of whom were found after the battle dead in their foxholes. The next morning, as tanks of the Third Carabiniers joined Durham in support of the advancing infantry, a Japanese officer leaped from a tree onto the back of a tank while the tank commander, facing forward, was standing in the open turret. The Japanese beheaded the commander with one swing of his sword, shoved the lifeless body aside, scrambled down into the tank, and stabbed its gunner to death. The attacker was after the gunner's pistol when the tank's driver beat him to it and shot him.

On the morning of February 28 a stripped-down fighting force began probing Meiktila's western defenses. At the same time Maj. Gen. David Tennant Cowan, commanding the 255th Tank Brigade and two infantry battalions with an artillery battery, swept around the city to the east and thrust into the jaws of its defenses. He was met by a fanatical enemy who unleashed artillery, machine guns, antitank fire, and snipers. As darkness fell on the first day the Japanese attempted to infiltrate the British-held zones, and hand-to-hand fighting raged the entire night.

The next day Slim persuaded an American general who had at his disposal a Mitchell bomber to fly him into Meiktila after his own Royal Air Force had refused the trip because it was too dangerous. Once there Slim witnessed firsthand some of the bitterest fighting of the four-day battle and ate his first Japanese-provided meal of biscuits and tinned food from a captured store. "It was not very good," he observed. He gave a much more favorable review of Cowan and his divisional commanders. He wrote later in his book *Defeat into Victory,* "To watch a highly skilled, experienced, and resolute commander controlling a hard-fought battle is to see, not only a man triumphing over the highest mental and physical stresses, but an artist producing his effects in the most complicated and difficult of the arts."[15]

Still the curious general wanted to see more. He hadn't been near real fighting since he had been promoted to army commander, and he knew just the regiment he wanted to see in action: his old haunt, the one he had served with as a colonel.

Slim, the American general, and their small party watched one prong of the attack on Meiktila unfold from behind the wall of a pagoda high on a hill. Only yards before them a platoon of Gurkhas working with an Indian-manned tank cleared a Japanese bunker by fighting their way close enough for a three-man charge. As the assault team rose from their cover in unison and began their sprint, one Gurkha went down in a lifeless heap, but the other two raced forward, reaching the bunker's loopholes, and there fired into them point-blank with Tommy guns. The remaining Gurkhas ran up to the bunker and surrounded it. As its half-dozen inhabitants fled from the rear, Slim watched the Gurkhas gun them down and good-naturedly made light of their marksmanship.

Upon clearing the fortification, the platoon moved to the next point of resistance, unfortunately not far away. As the van departed, a rear party approached the secured position to tend to the injured and search the dead Japanese and the bunker for IDs and documents. The attack filled Slim with pride, and he pronounced upon his men a high military compliment. The deadly task, he said, was proficiently carried out and was "all very businesslike."[16]

Every inch of Meiktila had to be taken in this fashion over the next three days. According to Slim, "every house was a strong point, every water channel had its concealed bunker and every rubble heap its hidden machine or antitank gun."[17] The fighting on March 2 and 3 was equally intense, and the relentless Japanese were killed where they fought, never giving an inch. Then, on the evening of March 3, fifty Japanese plunged into Lake Meiktila in the middle of town, a lake that legend held was dammed 2,500 years earlier by the grandfather of Gautama Buddha.[18] The Japanese soldiers who didn't drown were shot in the water like rats.[19]

Finally, having paid a gory price, the British controlled the shambles of Meiktila. Most important, they had cut the Japanese Army in half and formed the anvil upon which Slim intended to pound the hammer of his northern corps into Kimura's desperate attempt to retake the city.

Kimura's counterattack was fierce and bold, but the commander in charge, Lt. Gen. Honda Masaki, continually repeated a mistake that Slim had noted many times before with the Japanese. As the flexible Kimura reassigned units to retake Meiktila, their arrival, by necessity, was a staggered affair, with some arriving sooner than others. Instead of waiting until he had a critical mass of troops to effect an attack, Honda simply threw the new arrivals into battle as soon as they were available, thus defusing their impact. Nevertheless Kimura's counterattack was a do-or-die effort, and all involved knew it.

Honda attempted to cut Slim's vulnerable supply line and managed to retake the hills near Taungtha, closing the road to Meiktila. But the Japanese were devastated after four days of fighting, and soon supplies were moving down the Irrawaddy in boats; the British had even begun moving freight from the river port town of Myingyan to Meiktila on the local railroad. By the last week of March 1945, Meiktila was firmly in British hands and the final battle for central Burma, what Kimura had called "the Battle of the Irrawaddy Shore," was left to conclude forty-five miles to the north at Mandalay.

As the concurrent battles at Meiktila and Mandalay progressed, Slim took quick stock of his overall position. His central force, the Fourteenth Army, was making progress, but both flanks were stalled. His northern or left flank was mostly in the hands of the Americans and Chinese, whose problems were noted earlier. His southern or right flank in the Arakan, XV Corps, had stalled, and the Japanese were in strong positions blocking most routes of advance through the difficult, swampy country. Part of Slim's difficulty in the south was that he chose to limit air supply because he thought it better used in support of the central front. Finally, after considering all his options, he realized that his central front would be the only place where he would be able to make the necessary progress in the limited time. As he put it in his Operational Instruction of February 27, 1945:

(a) Destroy the Japanese forces in the Mandalay area.

(b) Seize Rangoon before the monsoon.[20]

The day before, Slim had unleashed the Nineteenth Division to storm down the great river's valley toward Mandalay, forty-five miles to the south. They moved like a torrent, "a rush of waters over a broken dam," and by March 3 they were in country where they could rightly deploy their tanks.[21] Resistance was at times stiff but was also reported to be uncoordinated. By March 8 they were fighting two miles east of the Mandalay cantonment and in the northern outskirts of the city. As outlying Japanese defenses gave way, the Battle for Mandalay was soon concentrated in two locations, Mandalay Hill in the northeastern quadrant of the town and Fort Dufferin in Mandalay city proper.

Mandalay Hill, northeast of the cantonment near the Irrawaddy, rose 800 feet above the surrounding plain and formed a natural watchtower for the city. On its steep sides was the Kuthodaw stupa, made up of 700 pagodas and temples that had contained hundreds of sacred white marble Buddhist tablets but which the Japanese now populated with machine guns and suicide squads.[22] March 9 saw the bloodiest fighting: all day long, dawn till dawn, Gurkhas stormed the defenders, Tommy-gunned their bunkers, used grenades at close quarters, and fought hand-to-hand. The Japanese never retreated. They were finished off, holding out in their cellars, when Slim's forces rolled petrol drums down on them and ignited their contents with tracer rounds.[23] By March 11 Mandalay Hill was in British hands. When Slim visited he could hear over the gunfire of the mopping-up operation a Welsh missionary hymn sung in the Khasi language of the advancing Assamese soldiers being led to their next fight by British general T. W. Rees, keeping time like a band leader at the head of their column.

Fort Dufferin was another sort of problem. Although the British were able to completely surround it, it was encased by thick stone walls covering embanked earth, and all around it ran a wide moat. It was a medieval sight indeed. It contained over a square mile of parks and gardens and the irreplaceable Teak Palace of Theebaw, the haunt of Burmese kings. On March 16 an attack on its northwest and northeast corners failed as the British were repulsed by heavy automatic fire. On the 18th and 19th four attempts to cross the moat failed.

Allied aircrews had bombed the fort's walls and fortifications with 500-pound munitions since the start of the siege while artillery pounded it with 5.5-inch shells, all to no avail. Slim called in Mitchell bombers armed with 2,000-pound munitions, which the resourceful Americans skip-bombed off the water of the moat to strike the walls directly. After several days they had pounded a fifteen-foot hole in the ramparts. General Slim, however, wisely decided that sending his men into the breach would be too costly. He reasoned that since the fort was an obstacle they could work around and it was "more, indeed, a matter of news value than military advantage," he prepared his forces to wait out the defenders.[24]

But on March 20, after the morning bombing runs, a group of Anglo-Burmese appeared at one of the gates, waving white flags and Union Jacks. They told the British the Japanese had snuck out the previous night through drains into the southern parts of Mandalay. When the British entered the fort, after defusing the multitude of booby traps left by the Japanese, they found themselves in possession of a great amount of stores and ammunition. General Rees raised the Union Jack over the fort, and a couple of days later Slim, as commander of the entire army and all the forces responsible for the victory, again raised the flag in a formal ceremony. Thus, after nearly three years of exile, Mandalay once again belonged to the British.

. . .

Other units of Slim's Fourteenth Army had met with success in the area around Mandalay. The lightning-fast Nineteenth Division had marched southeast over smugglers' trails for four days across two mountain ranges to capture Maymyo, the ancient summer capital of Burma. This cut the last rail line supplying troops opposing the remaining U.S. and Chinese forces in the north. In total the Nineteenth Division counted 6,000 enemy dead from battle encounters in Central Burma.[25]

On March 8 the Twentieth Division broke out to the south toward Kimura's new line of defense, where he had strung his Fifteenth, Thirty-third, and Twenty-eighth armies along a line drawn through Kyaukse, Myingyan Taungtha, Mount Popa, Kyaukpadaung, and Chauk. On March 16 they captured the railway at Myittha and cut the supply line for a main part of the remaining Japanese Army. By March 29 they attacked Kimura's defensive anchor town of Kyaukse, the place where the harried general had hoped to regroup his disorganized forces. Kyaukse fell the next day. In three weeks the Twentieth Division had swept the enemy from a forty-five-mile area, captured the Rangoon–Mandalay Railway, and left behind 2,000 dead Japanese. Kimura's Fifteenth and Thirty-first divisions were now, in Slim's words, "little more than groups of fugitives seeking refuge in the Shan Hills to the east."[26]

Slim's Second Division, which had been the last across the Irrawaddy, was five miles south of the river by March 6. As they fought their way south along the river's bank they first took Kyauktalon, then Myinthi, then Fort Ava, which guarded the Ava Bridge, a crossing destroyed by the British on their retreat from Burma in 1942. Their biggest coup came on March 20, when they occupied Amarapura and secured the expansive railway shops located there. The stores they captured were considerable, but their biggest score was the adjoining yard's treasure trove of rolling stock.

With central Burma as far south as Wundwin under his control and Kimura fighting stubbornly but without armor, guns, or transport, General Slim again took stock. His gambit had worked. Now he could see the way forward: the way to rid Burma of the Japanese once and for all was to "rush him [Kimura] off his feet before he could regain his balance—and pray for a late monsoon."[27]

31

The Home Fires

"Hey, where's that goon, anyway? This salami's almost ready and we've got no bread. We've only got one tub of impregnite, so I can't keep it hot all night." These, the worried words of Nels, head chef for the evening, lightened Jim's mood, as did the smell of frying salami in the aluminum mess kit and the stench of burning impregnite. The ambiance inside the tent was far from fine dining, but the end product, Jim knew, would be a delectable supplement to the evening's mess hall offering. After all, what passes for home cooking brings a smile to every household, right? Even when that household is 14,000 miles from your real household and the savory tones of frying salami are muted by the noxious bouquet of ester gum, neatsfoot oil, animal wax, paraffin wax, microcrystalline stearate, and Stoddard solvent, the currently oxidizing components of the ever versatile impregnite.[1]

Nels, wearing a stained white apron over his olive drabs, turned to Jim, raised his greasy spatula, and was about to say something when Herman Bisciani, a staff sergeant from Chicago off the Illinois Central, threw back the tent opening and announced to no one in particular, "Damn, those cooks were tight tonight. I could only talk them out of six slices of bread. But I got lots of butter and I got six beers from the PX." He put the goods on the footlocker near his cot and said, "Smells great in here."

Jim chuckled.

Tonight's postdinner entremet, a supplemental course to the camp cook's entrée of bean soup and cabbage, had traveled a long road before entering the frying pan. Marilou had mailed the four and a half pounds of tasty goodness from Klemm's German Butchery, at Jim's request, straight from good old Indianapolis. She had purchased the salami with Grandma Graf and dipped it in paraffin per Herr Klemm's suggestion. Thanks to the trusty postal service, both civilian and military, about three weeks later the cured, fermented, and air-dried sausage arrived in the boondocks of Bengal, India, where her husband and his tent mates were about to put it to good use. The tub of impregnite was a gift from Uncle Sam. Ubiquitous in the lives of soldiers it was intended to protect boots and to be used during chemical attacks, but placed between two bricks and ignited, it was a more than serviceable camp stove.

"Let's get this show on the road. Who's first?" Nels asked of the two other sergeants. Herman was busy pulling the tab on a can of beer so Jim was the first to grab a slice, load it with butter, and present it to Nels for the sizzling coup de grace. Grease dripped from the hoisted meat just as it landed on the buttery cushion of the white bread.

As the three men sat on their respective cots and ate their evening's rewards they critiqued the sausage and agreed it was "a good one." They talked with their mouths full. During second beers the mood became reflective, and discussion turned to loved ones. Nels and Herman had their own bedevilments on the home front, but they knew that Jim's situation was more worrisome. So they hedged their conversation and only indirectly coaxed Jim to talk. Herman finally glanced over at Nels, who raised his eyebrows ever so slightly, then switched to the direct approach. Herman asked, "What are you going to do, Jim? I'm damn near sure you'd qualify for a hardship release, if you apply. I saw one come through HQ the other day and the fellow had less to claim than you do. I can get the paperwork started. You're going to need some letters from home. Is Marilou up and around? Can she . . ."

Jim held up his right hand in a stop signal and said hesitantly, "Thanks, Herm, I know you guys will help, but I need a little longer to think about this. Thanks."

And with that, the conversation moved back into neutral territory, and the three tent mates yammered about less consequential matters until it was time for lights out.

32

Blue Flag

"What happened to this thing, Sarge?" asked a perplexed Alvin Carder, pointing to a dead locomotive with a blue flag attached to its lead handrail. The ailing unit was being shoved past him into the shop by the second-trick yard crew for repairs.

Over the screeching of steel wheels on the sharp curve of the engine house lead, Jim Hantzis yelled back, "You'd never guess" and handed the shop order to Carder. After the engine passed Carder read out loud:

> While underway to Station Lalmanirhat from Parbatipur Yards, locomotive was proceeding normally after taking on fuel and water at Rangpur, Milepost 195½. Engine suffered suspected injector failure near Mohendranagar at Milepost 176¾ and came to a halt where the boiler fire was extinguished. Upon further investigation, the water boiler injectors were determined to be in proper working order but the water supply had been depleted. This unexpected problem was caused by one large male pachyderm being transported in an elephant car first out behind the tender. The beast managed to work free the manhole covering the water reservoir located on the right rear corner of the tender car, drain approximately 1,000 gallons of water using his trunk and make for himself a presumably refreshing shower.[1]

Carder handed the shop order back to Sergeant Hantzis, took off his short-billed cap, and scratched his head. Returning his cap to his head, he tucked the bill and said to no one in particular, "Just another day at the zoo."

33

Coupled Up

E. O. Woods, an engineer from Syracuse, New York, slowly backed the locomotive and tender down the lead track off the main line to Katihar. The cut of fifty-one cars that would make up their train was in Track 4. The young engineer leaned out the locomotive's right-side window and watched as the head brakeman, Don Blair from Nassau, New York, threw the lead switch to line them up for a coupling.

The brakeman dogged the uncooperative switch catch using the weight of his right foot. Using New York Central hand signals, he began circling his right arm in the direction of E.O., all the time walking carefully toward the open knuckle of the first car over uneven ballast littered with debris, oil spills, chunks of coal, and rotting grain. As the tender's coupler neared the cut of cars the brakeman's circling stopped and his signal changed to a flat horizontal wave perpendicular to the movement of the engine and tender.

At this signal E.O. stopped the engine with about a car's length left between the couplers. The brakeman stepped into the center of the track behind the tender car and aligned the massive coupler that rode about three feet above the ground on its greasy slide. He cradled the heavy steel device in his arms at gut level and gave it a heave so that it was centered parallel to the tracks. Then he stepped back outside of the track, into E.O.'s view, and with his gloved right hand lifted the long arm on the side of the tender to release the coupling pin locking the knuckle in the closed position. The pin was uncooperative and required three heavy yanks on the long arm before it caught and opened. When the pin released the knuckle parted ever so slightly, like a fist just starting to open.

Don stepped between the tracks and reached in to fully open

the knuckle, then stepped back into E.O.'s view. Satisfied that the tender was lined up and ready, Don walked to the lead car in the cut, a petroleum tanker, and performed the same operation on its coupling device.

Don thought about how in the States under normal circumstances having a tanker full of gasoline first out in a cut would have been a safety violation. But this wasn't the States and the circumstances weren't normal.

When Don was satisfied that both pieces of equipment were properly lined up and ready for coupling he stepped from between the tracks back into E.O.'s view and gave him a small circling signal with his arm raised at a forty-five-degree angle. At this E.O. started backing up slowly. When the tender was about twenty feet from the cut of cars Don's signal changed to a high, wide arc made above his head that grew shorter as the distance between the equipment narrowed. When the two couplers touched, Don let his arm drop to his waist and made a fast horizontal stop signal perpendicular to the movement.

As contact was made Don watched to make sure that both pins dropped into their locked positions. Satisfied that the pins had fallen and the coupling was solid he looked up at E.O. and crossed his arms above his head. This meant he was about to step into the narrow space between the cars, about double the width of his shoulders, and couple the air hoses. E.O. acknowledged Don's move with a quick, low note of the whistle.

To make the coupling Don would have to drop to one knee between the tender car and the tanker. The joint would be made in the space under the couplers, just above the track bed. During this maneuver Don would be especially vulnerable; he would be unable to react fast enough to movement in the equipment to keep from being run over.

E.O. understood the danger. He set the engine and tender brakes so that if anything unexpected happen at the other end of the cut, such as a car mistakenly being switched into the cut or slack running out, the engine and tender would act as an anchor, limit the sudden movement, and perhaps save Don's life.

Don dropped to his right knee and grabbed the tender car's air hose with his right hand. With his left hand he forced the heavy rubber line to crimp about halfway along its three-foot length and transferred the bent section to his right hand. He reached under the drawbars, grabbed the hose from the tanker car with his left hand, and lifted both sections almost to the bottom of the drawbars. He let the two couplers slip together in a downward motion so their grooves interlocked and their rubber seals meshed. When he was finished the joined hoses took the form of the letter "U" crossing under the drawbars of the tender and tanker. The bottom of the U rode about a foot and a half above the track bed. Don smacked the top of the joint with the heel of his right hand to make sure the two hoses were locked, then rose from his right knee.

Now that the air hoses were connected Don had to line the angle cocks. Angle cocks are valves at the ends of each piece of rolling stock equipped with air brakes; they are mounted at the base of each rubber air hose and control air flow through the train line. For air to flow the full length of the train line, he would need to make sure that both the cock on the tender and the cock on the tanker were in the open or lined position.

Angle cocks are always on the right side of equipment looking square at the end. Don saw that the cock on the tanker, on the other side of the connected drawbars, was already open; that is, the cock valve was lined straight with the air hose. He also noticed that the tanker's wheels were chocked forward with a two-foot piece of splintered, grayish wood, that the pistons on the air brakes were in and not extended, and that the chain linking the handbrake to the brake rod was taut. These bits of information told the brakeman that the cars in the cut had no air pressure and had been bled off. Thus they were free to roll at any time for any reason. They had been parked with a chock in the downhill direction and a hand-brake applied to prevent them from accidentally rolling out of the departure yards onto the switching lead and then onto the main line. Should that unfortunate but all too frequent event occur, the free-rolling cars would be designated a runaway.

Don reached for the angle cock on the tender car with his right hand. The valve was in the closed position with the cock at a right angle to the train line. He was careful to gently open the cock to prevent a sudden depressurization that would cause the system to "go into the big hole." The valve was sticky and he had to strike it with the palm of his right hand in measured blows until it was lined with the air hose. He could hear the air rushing though the system as it opened wider.

He stepped back into E.O.'s view and gave him a thumbs-up signal. An instant later E.O. began carefully dumping air into the braking system with a gradual forward motion of the locomotive's feed valve.

Don lifted his right foot two feet off the ballast into the tanker's oily stirrup and simultaneously grabbed the equally oily horizontal handrail at chest level. With a heavy lunge off his left leg and a knee-popping lift from his right he awkwardly climbed onto the car's grated steel platform to release the handbrake.

Don hated tankers and muttered a curse under his breath as he tried to torque the big steel wheel clockwise, all the time kicking at the clumsy foot lock to get the brake to release. He had hurt his back and come close to falling and getting run over while working on this poorly designed equipment too many times to remember. It was bad enough trying to mount a tanker standing still, but while it was moving, at night, maybe during a storm, the equipment was outright deadly.

When the wheel wouldn't budge Don knew it was because the yard brakeman had applied the handbrake with the aid of a brake club, a three-foot section of hardwood lumber inserted between the spokes of the brake wheel for leverage. Don muttered another curse and dismounted the tanker. He walked to the engine, climbed the steep steps into the cabin, and retrieved a club from beside the fireman's seat. E.O. asked, "Problem with the brakes?"

"The yard crew must have used a gorilla to tie down that car."

"Some of those guys on third trick look like gorillas."

Don chuckled low under his breath.

The brakeman returned to the tanker, remounted it, and using the club for leverage, knocked off the hand brake. The first six cars in the cut were all tankers, so he repeated the brake release routine on each one.

Tying brakes on two cars was standard procedure for a cut of this length. Had the lead cars been empty, they might have tied down three, but these cars were full of good, old-fashioned, highly explosive gasoline bound for thirsty trucks and Jeeps and airplanes.

Don dismounted the second tanker and, after kicking the chock from the first tanker's wheel, again walked toward the engine. Without thinking he held the brake club in his right hand and used it as a hiking staff as he negotiated the uneven ballast.

E.O. watched the big round train line gauge slowly climb toward the prescribed 70 pounds per square inch. At this pressure the piston rods of the air brakes on the first twelve cars, the only cars of their sixty-car train with air-braking capacity, would extend outward from their cylinders and through an elaborate mechanical rigging of pivots, beams, and levers release the asbestos brake blocks from contact with the rolling surface of the wheels.

Getting a feel for a train's braking system was something a good engineer took pride in. Crappy braking was something train crews and machinists cussed. E.O. was one of the best engineers in the battalion. He knew his braking, and he didn't panic, two facts greatly appreciated by Don and the rest of the crew.

But braking in India had its own set of problems. They were twofold. First, not all the cars in the train had brakes; thus the braking duties of the cars with brakes were increased. This meant that to make a service application the train line pressure had to be drawn down dangerously close to the big hole. This concern didn't escape the crew, so when the train was in motion, no one stood up without holding onto something, just in case.

Operating with partial braking also meant that should a knuckle break, a not uncommon event, the train would separate into two sections and the separated section would become a runaway. Of course the separated section would probably have attached on its far end the caboose with a GI crew inside and maybe some Indian transits along for a cheap ride.

The second problem was that most of the Indian equipment

used vacuum braking, an entirely different braking system than the Americans used. By World War II all the large American railroads were using the more technologically advanced Westinghouse air brake system primarily because the Americans ran longer and heavier trains. E.O., Don, and the rest of the crew were lucky to be dispatched on an air brake train. At least operating the brakes would be somewhat familiar and one less thing to worry about.

Don entered the cabin and sat down in the fireman's seat. He was nervous about their trip but, like E.O., didn't want it to show. More of a talker than E.O., he began chatting about last evening's chow and the lack of fresh green beans. Don loved fresh green beans, especially the way his mother made them, with bacon, tomatoes, onions, and garlic. He loved them with thick, almost pasty but not lumpy mashed potatoes whipped with lots of butter. The dehydrated spuds they got in camp were edible but not, E.O. learned, in the same league as Don's mother's potatoes.

Then Don started talking about how, in just a couple of weeks, his mom would need him to till the family's garden plot back in Nassau so that she could plant her new crop of green beans and that those plants would be loaded with their first picking by early July if the weather was right.

Don was talking to no one in particular and rambling on when a thundery, guttural, metallic bang rang out from somewhere in the classification yards about a quarter-mile away. E.O. rose from his seat and crossed the cabin to join Don and look out the window. Both men searched the yards in the direction of the sound. Seeing no smoke E.O. finally said, "I guess they're just switching cars. It must have been a heavy coupling. Nothing's on fire over there."

Don agreed. "Yeah, I guess you're right."

Crossing back to his seat, E.O. said, "That first-trick yard job's probably still getting used to the equipment and the roll."

Don fell silent for a moment. Then, with new earnestness, he looked at E.O. and asked, "Have you ever thought how easy it would be to shoot a railroad train?"

E.O. registered the change of subject with a quizzical glance.

Don went on without E.O. saying a word. "I mean, if you're in an airplane and you want to shoot a railroad train, all you have to do is find a railroad. And how hard can that be? You fly until you run across a railroad track, then you follow it in either direction and, eventually, you'll find a railroad train. Just look for the smoke. Hell, even the Japs can figure that out.

"Then, once you find a train, what's the train going to do? Shoot back? Run and hide? Swerve and dodge? If you're the pilot you know exactly where to lead the shot because where the tracks go is where the train's going. There's no sport in it. Shooting trains should be outlawed. It should be its own Geneva Convention!

"And blowing up tracks and booby-trapping bridges? I mean, where's the sport? Hell, they could even sink us on a barge in this operation. Sink a railroad train, now there's a new twist."

E.O. held up his left hand in a stop gesture and shook his head at Don. With a low chuckle he said, "That'll do, that'll do," using railroad lingo for "Stop." He pointed to the steaming tea billy above the firebox door and told the young brakeman in a reassuring voice, "Have some of Darjeeling's finest. It's like Champagne in the morning. It'll calm your nerves."

34

The New President

Once again the GIs found themselves huddled around the radio. President Roosevelt had died in Warm Springs, Georgia, on April 12, 1945. The news had been released to the public just before that evening's network news broadcasts. He'd been sitting for a portrait when stricken.

It was solemn in the usually noisy mess hall. So interwoven was the personal with the political that one young private from Company B told his sergeant, Jim Hantzis, "President Roosevelt was like a relative to me, Sarge. Like an uncle, I guess. I was only nine years old when he became president, and he's the only one I've ever known. What you think is gonna happen now?"

Jim, himself only twenty-five, could barely remember FDR's predecessor, Herbert Hoover, who left office in March 1933. "Truman's a military man. He'll know what to do," he told the young private. "The shame of it is that FDR won't be around to see us win."

Sergeant Hantzis was right about the new president. He did know what to do. He had fourteen million men and women under arms and an enemy in the Pacific that had time and again shown they would fight to the last man standing. Although he had just learned of the atomic bomb, no one could tell him for certain that it would work or when it would be ready to deploy. From President Truman's standpoint, he was about to ask three to four million soldiers, sailors, marines, and airmen to undertake the largest invasion in history against a land that had never in its unimaginably long history fallen to foreigners. According to estimates, he was about to order the death of between 500,000 and a million Americans, their lives to be paid as the price of invading, defeating, and occupying the Japanese home islands.[1] The date for the landing on Kyushu, the first of two invasion points, had been set for the first week of November 1945.

The new president was grimly realistic. American losses in the Pacific for the previous year had been over 200,000 dead and wounded, lost and missing. Ten thousand Americans were dead in the Marianas, 5,500 dead at Leyte, 9,000 in the Luzon campaign, 6,800 at Iwo Jima, 12,600 at Okinawa, and 2,000 killed on tiny Peleliu in the Palau group of islands.[2] Since Pearl Harbor, the United States had lost at least 1,252,000 personnel to combat-related causes, and this number did not include losses due to disease.[3]

As Truman made ready to introduce himself to the soldiers he would command, he knew that one out of every seven he was about to address would probably be dead in six months, and many times that number torn by the wounds of war. Of the servicemen he would order to invade Japan, the war-weary but resolved nation would probably lose one in three.

"All of us have lost a great leader, a far-sighted statesman and a real friend of democracy," Truman declared. "We have lost a hard-hitting chief and an old friend of the services.

"Our hearts are heavy. However, the cause, which claimed Roosevelt, also claims us. He never faltered—nor will we!

"I have done, as you do in the field, when the Commander in Chief falls. My duties and responsibilities are clear. I have assumed them. These duties will be carried on in keeping with our American tradition.

"As a veteran of the First World War, I have seen death on the battlefield. When I fought in France with the Thirty-fifth Division, I saw good officers and men fall, and be replaced.

"I know the strain, the mud, the misery, the utter weariness of the soldier in the field. And I know too his courage, his stamina, his faith in his comrades, his country and himself.

"We are depending upon each and every one of you."

The new president sought to go beyond the transition at hand and express the resolve of the great nation: "At this decisive hour in history it is very difficult to express my feeling. Words will not convey what is in my heart.

"Yet, I recall the words of Lincoln, a man who had enough eloquence to speak for all America. To indicate my sentiments, and to describe my hope for the future, may I quote the immortal words of that great Commander in Chief: 'With malice toward none; with charity for all; with firmness in the right, as God gives us to see the right, let us strive on to finish the work we are in; to bind up our nation's wounds; to care for him who shall have borne the battle, and for his widow, and his orphan—to do all which may achieve and cherish a just and lasting peace among ourselves, and with all nations.'"

When the brief broadcast concluded the battalion's commander signaled for the radio to be turned off and simply said to all those assembled, "Carry on, men."

. . .

For the 721st Railway Operating Battalion "carrying on" was getting easier. The work remained hard, but at least the amenities available in camp were improving. Best of all, the men were enjoying one day a week off work. Thanks to the British taking over the responsibility of operating the captured railways in Burma, the U.S. Army's Sixty-first Composite Group disbanded in February 1945 and redeployed to Parbatipur in March. The Composite Group's soldier railroaders lightened the load of the 721st. Rest leaves and three-day passes were granted more frequently as well.[4]

There was a common notion among the GIs that, given the leash and leeway, they could improve anything. In that vein the Signal Corps of H&S Company wired every tent and building in camp for electricity and supplied the current from three diesel generators. Company A's trackmen found time from their work building sidings, a tremendous aid to the flow of traffic on the railroad, and supervised paving the streets in camp.[5] This welcome project eliminated the dreadful mud and muck that sapped so much time and energy.

Pipefitters and welders from Company B set up a boiler to provide steam pressure for the kitchen and, to everyone's great delight, hot water for the showers. The theater got an enclosed stage, the dispensary got a hospital room, a camp bakery was added, and there was more stock in the Post Exchange. In just a couple of weeks the GIs would get a brand new Servicemen's Club sponsored by the Red Cross. The writing desks, comfortable chairs, phonograph, Ping-Pong tables, and library would be almost as welcome as the young American women who staffed it.

But difficult and dangerous work went on amid the new luxury. In mid-February Company B completed the conversion of seventy-five War Department flat cars into logging cars.[6] Each new car received wooden ends reinforced by angle iron braces, which were riveted and welded into position. With the car's ends in place, the men fitted four wooden stakes on each side and ran two lengths of half-inch and quarter-inch chain through iron brackets on the side sills to prevent the loads shifting laterally. They used a diesel-powered air compressor made by Ingersoll Rand to run their pneumatic drills, riveting guns, and saws. With the help of these power tools and by organizing their work in an assembly-line fashion the men were able to complete the conversion in twelve days.

Along with the daily inspection of all locomotives the men of Company B started converting all the rolling stock to American-style vacuum brake systems. By the end of March 1945 they had upgraded over 400 units. This conversion required that each piece of equipment be fitted with compatible vacuum reservoirs and cylinders. Each cylinder had to be disassembled and have a rolling ring and end gasket installed. Then the reassembled cylinders were mounted under the cars. The reservoirs also had to be mounted and connected to vacuum lines and cylinders by flexible hose. With the vacuum system in place, brake components were installed in proper alignment, the brake piston travel checked, the linkage adjusted, and the whole system checked for leaks. Once the men were certain all connections were air-tight, they riveted or welded on a swan's neck to both ends of the car and on it mounted the vacuum hose that coupled cars together. Finally they stenciled a test date on the reservoir.

Each newly appointed wagon was then switched out from the car shop to Track 11 in the Parbatipur South Yards, where the brakes got a rolling test and final adjustments were made. With a stamp of approval the equipment was released for service. Thanks to the new braking system, the cars could handle increased tonnage, faster track speeds, and be combined with more cars like them for longer trains. Altogether the vacuum brake conversion made for safer, faster, and more efficient movement of freight. And that in a nutshell was what the American operation of the Bengal and Assam Railroad was all about.

But of all the shop projects the one that made the men of Company B proudest was converting flat cars to low-sided gondolas. This was a big project. Each car had to have its ends fashioned from salvaged lumber since the materials for this work were often in short supply. And since most of the flat cars arrived without stake pockets on their sides, the men had to attach sixteen per car, eight a side. This required the drilling and reaming of sixty-five holes per car plus twenty-four holes for the corner braces, for a total of eighty-nine holes through the heavy steel rolling stock. The stake pocket brackets, fashioned from steel strips in a separate manufacturing line, were secured to the cars with rivets from a gun powered by an oil heater and the company's much prized air compressor. When, in mid-March 1945, Company B had completed the conversion of 676 flat cars, the men looked back with pride on the sweat and teamwork that had made it possible to finish—on average—one car every fifteen minutes.[7]

35

Endgame

General Slim had rightly anticipated the endgame. Rangoon, the city whose name means "the end of the war," was the target of Slim's initial southward scramble. It was toward there that his Fourteenth Army was hell-bent. But cagey Kimura and his forces became a moving target, and he would be the one to set in motion the final gambit.[1]

Slim had left Kimura's forces bloodied and scattered following Meiktila and Mandalay. After that the best Kimura could muster was a weak west-to-east line of defense running from Yenang-yaung to Pyawbwe, twenty miles south of Meiktila. Beyond that line Rangoon lay 300 miles south by rail and 350 by river.[2] As Slim took stock in mid-March 1945 he assumed the monsoon would break around May 15. That gave him forty days at best, after he had cleared the remaining enemy from his rear, to move into position, attack, and capture Rangoon. Short of that he would be left with a very large army in need of very many supplies at the beginning of a monsoon with no route of withdrawal.

Slim's tank and motorized transport losses in the battles for Meiktila and Mandalay had been manageable, but their equipment was in need of repair and maintenance. Everything depended upon his army's ability to hit hard and fast with its armored spearhead. The men, however, were in a fit and fighting mood and determined to keep the equipment running. Slim told one tank and armored car unit that when he gave the word to begin the dash to Rangoon, "every tank they had must be a starter, and every tank that crossed the starting line must pass the post in Rangoon. After that they could push them into the sea if they wanted!"[3]

Of the two routes southward Slim chose the railway for the main attack force. A smaller grouping would move down the Irrawaddy

River Valley, covering both sides of the river, drawing off Japanese from the main force, and providing the general with another column to strike with if needed. Slim had at his disposal seven divisions, but two would have to return to India because of the difficulty of supplying them. Of the five remaining only three, along with two tank brigades, could be supplied by air, thus giving them the capability of swift movement along the route of advance. Slim decided it would be these units, traveling along the railroad, that would lead the charge to Rangoon. The IV Corps, currently at Meiktila and already forty miles south of the other units, was mostly on a mechanized and airborne establishment. They would highball to Rangoon. XXXIII Corps would move down the Irrawaddy.[4]

So, "having kicked over the anthill; the ants running about in confusion," Slim had some tidying up to do before he could launch southward. As he planned a strike at Pyawbwe to clear the route to Rangoon, he receive news that Aung San, the Burman who the Japanese had placed in charge of the country's puppet military, the Burma National Army, was ready to defect and bring along the bulk of his fighting forces. "The B.N.A. prowling on their lines of communication, cutting an occasional throat, ambushing small parties, would give the Japanese an uncomfortable feeling on dark nights," he later wrote.[5]

Kimura planned to hold Slim as far from Rangoon as possible. He sent the Thirty-third Army to stop the advance down the railway at Pyawbwe and the Twenty-eighth Army to contain the forces moving down the Irrawaddy north of Yenangyaung. Meanwhile Slim was behind schedule mopping up Japanese resistance around Kyaukse. Worried about taking Rangoon before the monsoon, he once again lobbied for an amphibious assault to enhance his land attacks.

An attack from sea, complemented by airborne units, had been drawn up as an operational possibility back in November 1944. At that time it was known as Plan Z. But Churchill had warned Mountbatten when they met in Cairo a month before that the Germans were putting up a stiffer fight than expected and that the equipment for the landing might not be ready.[6] When Slim signaled his disinterest in the plan because it would have tied up precious air support for his Fourteenth Army, the option was pulled from the table. Now, after a heart-to-heart with Admiral Mountbatten, the landing was ordered under the codename Operation Dracula to coincide with Slim's arrival at Rangoon.

The fight for control of the Irrawaddy River Valley began to take shape around Taungdwingyi, about sixty miles southeast of Meiktila. But the Japanese commander, Sakurai Shozo, made two unrecoverable mistakes. He underestimated the speed of the British units, and he left the town garrisoned by Indian National Army units and Japanese administrative troops. Sakurai was spellbound when, on April 14, a mechanized brigade seized the town. Only four days earlier the nearest British units were in Meiktila. In fact not only was he surprised; he was in denial. He kept sending convoys through Taungdwingyi for the next few days, as Slim says, "to the great profit and entertainment of the Twentieth Division."[7] The Indian National Army once again melted under pressure, and on April 18 an armored column sank three boatloads of fleeing Japanese on the Irrawaddy. By April 22, the Seventh Division had advanced downriver on both banks and occupied Yenangyaung with all of its oil fields intact and took possession of many abandoned Japanese vehicles in good running order.

By April 28 the advance down the Irrawaddy was at Allanmyo, and on May 1 XXXIII Corps established its headquarters at Magwe. Along the way the retreating Japanese left behind not only towns and strong points but much of their discipline as well. The advancing British units found villagers and peasants tied to trees and bayoneted; as Slim noted, if their morale was gone, their savagery remained.

As the British Seventeenth Division began to probe southward from Meiktila they ran into stiff resistance at Yindaw, ten miles north of Pyawbwe. They found themselves up against a permanent, well-planned line of defense, massed antitank guns, artillery, obstacles to impede movement, and mines galore.[8] The fight for Yindaw would take precious time away from the capture of Pyawbwe and the much-anticipated sprint to Rangoon. So on April

18, the Seventeenth Division bypassed Yindaw and left it to the Fifth Division to deal with later. The spearhead then moved on to Pyawbwe, where two days later they engaged the main strength of the enemy line.

After a nighttime tank-to-tank battle, hand-to-hand combat, and one assault after another the Japanese line began to give. When British units maneuvered to the Japanese rear and let loose an armored thrust, Lieutenant General Honda's defenses collapsed. The advancing forces had no idea how successful they had been. They had Honda and the whole Thirty-third Army's headquarters in their sights. Honda was crouched in a foxhole writing his will when the British broke off the attack on what to them seemed like an inconsequential secondary objective. No one had told them of the prize within their grasp because no one knew.[9] The British counted 2,000 Japanese dead in the town and captured and killed many more fleeing. The battle was decisive: it destroyed Honda's army and, according to General Slim, settled the fate of Rangoon as well.[10]

With the roadblock removed it was as if a starter had fired his pistol and the sprint was on. Early on the morning of April 11, Seventeenth Division and Fifth Division filed past their proud commander southbound on the road to Rangoon. General Slim saw "an air of purpose about every truck that rolled dustily by." He talked with the commander of Fifth Division, Brig. Robert Mansergh, and reported, "Fresh, alert, and eager, he somehow, for a flash, made me think of the start of a dawn duck shoot in India."[11]

On April 24 Slim learned that Kimura was retreating from his headquarters in Rangoon to Moulmein, across the Bay of Moutama, sixty miles from the border with Thailand. Kimura was leaving himself an escape route. He had to retreat overland because going by sea meant that if the British Navy didn't get him, the monsoon would. But the overland route took him through Pegu, and whoever controlled that gateway would win the last race in Burma.

Slim wasn't sure if Kimura had cleared Rangoon. He feared that the Japanese would leave behind a suicide garrison and try to hold him out until the rains. But Kimura had left in a very unconventional manner; he declined to issue written orders for his men to leave because his orders from Supreme Commander Terauchi Hisaichi were to hold southern Burma at all cost. Kimura's *interpretation* of that order was that it could not be accomplished in Rangoon and had to be done from Pegu. So, unknown to Slim, Rangoon was quickly coming unglued, and the remaining Japanese were on their own to find their way to Pegu. After Kimura left, no one thought it a good idea to stay.

Meanwhile Kimura called for all available Japanese troops to concentrate at Pegu, a big town that straddled the banks of the river for which it was named. It was home to a 200-foot-long statue of Buddha reclining and many pagodas.

On the morning of April 29, General Cowan, commander of Seventeenth Division, launched the attack on Pegu from the north, east, and southeast. The fighting was as intense and bitter as any in the war, and by the next day the British had won the battle for the demolished railroad bridges. But as night fell on April 30, they had yet to dislodge the Japanese from the roadway bridge. Cowan would not be ready to advance on Rangoon until May 2.

On May 1 the skies opened two weeks before the date Slim had prayed for. The onset of the monsoon immobilized IV Corps, which had just secured Pegu and was making ready to take Rangoon. The rains continued through the night, and the roads quickly became impassable, the streams swelled, and the bridges washed away. General Slim had lost the race against the rain but won the Battle for Burma.

36

Above Rangoon Jail

"EXDIGITATE," read the hand-painted sign visible from the air far above. That was British airmen's slang for "Remove your thumb from your ass and get on with it." As he flew above the Rangoon Jail four miles north of the Burmese capital, Wing Commander A. E. Saunders chuckled to himself under the roar of the Mosquito's twin Packard Merlin 33s. "The bloke who wrote that certainly knows how to get someone's attention," he thought.[1] The flyboy phrase had prompted his hasty flight, and his trusty De Havilland Wooden Wonder hadn't failed him. Even with the early onset of the monsoon, the plane's plywood balsa spars and doped Madapolam fabric skin were still taut and secure. Most of the other Mosquitoes in 110 Squadron had already succumbed to Burma's punishment. They were rugged airplanes and sentimental favorites, but the forces of nature cannot be denied.

He flew on toward the Mingaladon airfield a few miles away. As he banked the agile reconnaissance bomber to the left for a better view of the runway, Saunders used the intercom to talk to the Mosquito's navigator, Flight Lieutenant James Stephen, seated to his right and slightly to the rear. The radio crackled and then cleared. Stephen could hear Saunders's tinny voice in his earphones: "I don't see a bloody airplane anywhere, no ground crews, no fueling lorries . . . not even a security detail. What'd you make of it, Lieutenant?"

"It jolly well looks like the little buggers have bid this place 'Sayonara,' commander," came back the navigator's response.

"Let's have a closer look at the runway, shall we?" Saunders said as he put the plane into a gradual descent.

The tarmac had been thoroughly bombed and cratered by Allied air attacks. "It's too rough to chance a landing," Saunders thought, again to himself. "But the message can't be a ruse. It's real. The Japs are gone. If I don't get to those poor bastards at the jail they'll be at the mercy of tomorrow's shelling."

He thought over the situation for only a second, then, with typical British understatement, warned the navigator, "Make ready to land, Lieutenant, we may be going in a tad botch."

As the lightweight plane touched the tarmac at over 100 knots its left landing gear took the first of many jolting blows. The right side seemed to ride better, but as they rolled to a stop with the tail wheel dragging, it was clear from the airplane's drooping list to the left that the Mosquito would not be taking off without repairs. And as far as Saunders knew, since he and his navigator were at that moment the only active-duty British combat personnel in Rangoon, repairs would not be forthcoming.

The two airmen set off on foot toward the Rangoon Jail. Just the day before reconnaissance aircraft photographing the city in preparation for its bombardment had spotted two messages. The first flyover photographed a Union Jack hoisted on the compound's flagpole and the words "JAPS GONE. BRITISH HERE" painted on the roof. After that morning's bombing sortie a second reconnaissance patrol caught on film the same message with the additional phrase "EXDIGITATE." It was that admonishment that convinced Saunders the message was legitimate and not another Japanese trick.[2]

Outside of the airfield's gates the two men hired an oxcart for the ride into the city. At the jail in deserted downtown Rangoon the two men were greeted by 1,400 prisoners of war, American, British, and Indian. Some had been incarcerated for more than three years. They explained to Saunders that two days earlier the Japanese had abandoned them while they slept. A prisoner had gone to the latrine in the middle of the night and found a note wedged into the window bars: "To the whole captured persons of Rangoon Jail. According to the Nippon Military Order, we hereby give you liberty to leave this place at your will. Regarding other materials kept in the compound, we give you permission to consume them as far as necessity is concerned. We hope that we shall have the opportunity to meet you again on the battlefield somewhere. We shall continue our war effort in order to get the emancipation of all Asiatic races."[3]

The prisoners had slaughtered a couple of hogs, eaten a great meal, and decided they had better warn their comrades of their predicament lest they be bombed along with the rest of the city. Painting their message on the roof and following it up with a fraternal exclamation had done the job, just in the nick of time.

That evening, after hearing the prisoners' story, Wing Commander Saunders walked to the Rangoon River. At the city docks he commandeered a sampan and, as darkness approached, set off downstream to the mouth of the muddy, rain-swollen waterway. There he met a flotilla of launches motoring upriver carrying the British Twenty-sixth Division, bayonets fixed and primed for their anticipated forced landing. Luckily theirs would be all landing and little force.

With the next day's bombardment called off, the Royal Air Force instead dropped Red Cross parcels and K-rations. The grateful ex-prisoners enjoyed chocolate and biscuits and the forgotten luxuries of chewing gum and cigarettes. They dressed their sores with new bandages and threw away the old scraps of rag and paper they had been using to keep the flies and insects off their wounds.[4] In just one more day, aboard the hospital ship *Karapara*, they would all take steaming hot baths—their first in three years.

And so Rangoon, the key to ruling Burma, threatening India, isolating China, and safeguarding Singapore and the Philippines, was captured on May 2 by a brave duo in a lonely wooden airplane that didn't fire a shot. With Rangoon in hand, the British now had to complete the expulsion of the Japanese from Burma and make ready to retake Malaya and Singapore. Their victory had won them a town and a country and left them at the end of a 900-mile-long line of communication stretching all the way back to the American railroad at Dimapur.

Their newly captured deepwater port at Rangoon was the key to their survival because Slim had forged one of the longest and narrowest salients in the history of war. His two main routes southward through Burma were more than 300 miles long and only a couple of miles wide. The general estimated, a bit low as it turned out, that the Japanese still had between 60,000 and 70,000 men west of his lines of communication, every single one of whom would try to cross to the east as if their life depended upon it, which it did.[5]

The bombed and demolished port facilities at Rangoon were put in working order in only six weeks through the nonstop efforts of the construction engineers. Of these men and the others in his supply chain, Slim had the highest regard. They were, to him, worthy of praise equal to that earned by his combat divisions. The 3,000 tons a day that began flowing through Rangoon during the monsoon would provision his troops and begin to supply a token of aid to the thirteen million Burmese whom he was now responsible for as well.[6]

Rebuilding the civil authority was another consuming task. The Japanese had taken with them many of the forced government servants of the old regime. Slowly, qualified personnel began to drift back into the population, and as they cleared security checks they were reappointed to suitable positions. A skeleton civil apparatus was up and running in about a month. Slim also negotiated a deal with Aung San and agreed to employ and ration the soldiers of the Burma National Army so long as they accepted orders from the British.[7]

Slim, like many of his soldiers and officers, had been away from England for a long time. He was suffering, as were they all, from "the soldier's dumb pain of separation."[8] On average most of his troops hadn't visited home for four to five years. Slim hadn't been home in seven. Confident that IV Corps could handle the enemy around Pegu and that XXXIII Corps would take care of any Japanese trying to cross the Irrawaddy, Slim went home for a month. While he was there the final battle of Burma took place.

. . .

The Battle of the Breakout was aptly named. Very simply, the Japanese tried to dash across Slim's lines twice, and both attempts failed miserably. On July 3 the Japanese Thirty-third Army with about 10,000 men tried to cross at Sittang. The battle and mopping up was fought in waist-deep marshland. Slim's Seventh Division held the only high ground to be had, and the results were as expected. On July 19 the remnants of the Japanese Twenty-eighth Army tried to run the gauntlet a bit farther north. The ones not killed in the fighting were drowned in the river. The final attempt to escape Burma was made by Japanese Naval Guard Forces, about 1,200 men. They made their dash on July 31; it was later learned that by August 4 only three sailors had managed to escape.[9]

As resistance in Burma came to an end, total Japanese casualties were estimated at 185,000 dead. The Battle for Burma was the Imperial Army's worst land defeat of the war.[10]

37

Germany Surrenders

Germany's surrender on May 8 rang throughout the GIs' world like chimes of freedom. Soldiers in Europe celebrated, drank wine with French women, danced in the streets with their Russian comrades, and wondered when they would be shipping east. Soldiers in the east, if they weren't being shot at, celebrated by staging mock captures, drinking beer, listening to music, and wondering when the guys in Europe would get there.

"Hitler never looked so good," Jim Hantzis said as he squinted through the viewfinder of the Kodak Brownie and clicked the shutter. "Why don't you guys rough him up a bit, you know, make it look a little more realistic?"

With that encouragement, Pvt. Joe Ward, off the L&N from Birmingham, Alabama, lunged for the cotton towel knotted around the otherwise naked waist of S.Sgt. Romelo Pavia from New York City, currently appearing in the lead role of a German tyrant without railroad affiliation.

Pavia, appropriately proportioned for his part as the diminutive dictator, dropped his right hand from his "Sieg Heil!" salute to protect his modesty. But in a truly inspired comical performance, he kept holding the upside-down toothbrush against his upper lip with his left hand, staying in character. Even though the most dangerous man on the planet, then being guarded by four GIs in combat gear, was fully surrounded, he managed an escape and was last seen fleeing down a row of tents with his mustache still in place, wearing boots, socks, and a freshly unknotted white bath towel. His last words were "Nein, nein, nein!" Even a star-struck, egomaniac dictator, it seems, fears some forms of embarrassment.

Hantzis never got the second picture, but the one he got was a keeper. It was a great picture for a great day.

The surrender signing took place at General Eisenhower's head-quarters in a redbrick schoolhouse in Rheims, in the Champagne region of France, on May 7. Two days later the Soviets had their surrender ceremony in a manor house serving as Red Army Head-quarters in Berlin. Marshal Zhukov signed for the USSR. Stalin considered the Rheims treaty to be a preliminary protocol to his, the true surrender document.

The Allies had received intelligence reports a week earlier that Hitler had killed himself. At the same time German radio was broadcasting that der Führer had died in battle. News of his suicide would not be released for many more days because nobody believed it. Allied intelligence agencies thought it was an escape ploy.

On May 8, at 9:00 a.m. Eastern War Time, President Tru-man told the American people, "The flags of freedom fly over all Europe." But lest anybody become too euphoric over the battle already won, he offered this prompt reminder on the battle yet to come:

> Our rejoicing is sobered and subdued by a supreme consciousness of the terrible price we have paid to rid the world of Hitler and his evil band. Let us not forget, my fellow Americans, the sorrow and the heartache which today abide in the homes of so many of our neighbors—neighbors whose most priceless possession has been rendered as a sacrifice to redeem our liberty.
>
> We can repay the debt, which we owe to our God, to our dead and to our children only by work—by ceaseless devotion to the responsi-bilities, which lie ahead of us. If I could give you a single watchword for the coming months, that word is—work, work, and more work.
>
> We must work to finish the war. Our victory is but half-won. The West is free, but the East is still in bondage to the treacherous tyr-anny of the Japanese. When the last Japanese division has surren-dered unconditionally, then only will our fighting job be done.[1]

As the flags flew, the bells tolled, and the people danced, for the moment all was happy and gay. Hantzis too was happy, swept up in the celebration in Parbatipur. But the frivolity, the posed photo, the liberal beer rations, and the high morale could lift him only so far. He had a lot on his mind. In a little over a month he would be granted a week-long pass and go to the rest camp at Madras with his buddy Stewart White. There, while the two enjoyed the swimming and saw the sights, Jim would make a difficult decision but one that he could not avoid.

. . .

Back in the United States the Hantzis family was in a downward spiral. Marilou had had a lumbar fusion operation in early April that left her out of work and in a hospital bed for six weeks. An even graver concern was the declining health of Gustav Graf, the seventy-four-year-old patriarch of the family and its primary wage earner; he had been diagnosed with liver cancer while Marilou was in the hospital, and now he was bedridden. His primary caregivers were his elderly wife and his recuperating granddaughter-in-law. To make things even worse, family members weren't discussing and planning for the financial and emotional challenges ahead. No one was in charge, and Marilou didn't want to overstep her bounds.

The two-story house on North Walcott in Indianapolis was home to Jim's mother and father, his four younger sisters, and the two grandparents. Since her wedding in June 1943 Marilou lived there as well. Normally everybody worked outside the house except for Jim's grandmother. Even the teenage daughters had afterschool jobs. But these were not normal times.

Jim knew this because Marilou dutifully wrote him with all the details. She massaged them with positive spins and constructive suggestions, but she didn't want to be the one to push the agenda. She didn't want to push the Hantzis family away from her. The oldest of seven children, Marilou was normally a take-charge person, and Jim could sense her frustration, fear, and uncertainty. It tore at him that he was so far away and unable to support the ones he loved.

He sent money home and he sent war bonds. In fact soon after he arrived in India he wrote to Marilou that he shouldn't need more than four or five dollars a month, so the rest of his $178 monthly salary went home. But all things considered, that was not enough to make up for the loss of Gustav's full-time railroad wages. Plus Jim and Marilou were trying to save for their life together after the war.

Marilou made $200 per month as assistant to Dr. George J. Garceau, who was chief of Orthopedic Services at St. Vincent Hospital in Indianapolis.[2] She was a well-paid registered nurse, the youngest of five physician's assistants in the city. But since her operation and prior traction treatment had prevented her from working, her income for the early months of 1945 was off, and she had been drawing from the kitty. Jim and Marilou had $50 together when they were first married. Since then they had put aside $1,454 in war bonds and savings, and it was in jeopardy.[3]

38

Discharge

"Your paperwork seems to be in order. Anything else you'd like to add, Sergeant?" asked Capt. Henry E. Owens.

"No, sir," replied the young man standing at ease before the company commander's desk.

"I'll need to finish processing the order and see what can be arranged for transportation. It could take a month or more just to get you out of here, but son, your request is approved. I hope you can help your family get back on their feet. You've done well here, Sergeant."

"Thank you, sir."

"You're dismissed," said the captain.

The young sergeant came to attention and saluted. The captain, still seated at his desk, returned the salute. Then Jim Hantzis did a sharp about-face and walked toward the door of Company B Headquarters. On his way through the outer office he bumped into his friend and fellow sergeant Nels Whittaker.

"How'd it go, Jim?" asked Nels in a low tone so none of the clerks could hear.

"He's cutting me loose," replied Jim.

"Well, it's for the best, buddy. How soon do you ship out?"

"He said it'll probably take a month."

"Hell, this whole shootin' match might be over in a month. You ain't gonna miss anything," said Nels. The fellow Hoosier added, "Looks like I'll be seeing you 'back home again in Indiana,'" singing the song's title as he patted Jim on his left shoulder.

. . .

"Sixteen hours ago an American airplane dropped one bomb on Hiroshima, Japan, and destroyed its usefulness to the enemy,"

President Truman announced on August 6. "That bomb had more power than twenty-thousand tons of TNT. It had more than two thousand times the blast power of the British Grand Slam, which is the largest bomb ever yet used in the history of warfare."[1]

And so the railroaders of the 721st learned about the atomic bomb. They were still celebrating a week later when Japan made its surrender official. When the celebration finally cooled, the first question on everyone's mind and asked repeatedly of every sergeant in the battalion was "When do we leave?"

39

The Conductor

9:30 p.m.
13 August 45

My Dearest Marilou:

Well darling here it is the thirteenth, don't ask me what happened on the twelfth, I don't remember. I can account for it up until about three o'clock in the afternoon, that's when I was packing and getting my records straight. But, around three the beer started flowing in the tent. Wow, the next thing I recall is at five o'clock this morning when I woke up. Of course, I can remember a few things but they're a bit hazy.

I'm getting to feel better now. We were drinking that airplane beer. You know, drink three and P-38. I'll tell you all about it later on.

Darling, it's another anniversary for us, only I'm a lot happier on this one than I have been for a long time. With lots of good luck I might be in the states for the next one.

I'm in Calcutta now. I left the 721st this morning and I'm staying here at the Red Cross tonight and tomorrow I report to camp. Darling, I don't know what to tell you about your writing me. After I reach camp tomorrow and find out what the prospects are for getting a boat, I'll let you know when to stop writing. You might write Time and the VFW magazines and have them start sending them to you. Also, you might write the Sunday Star and anyone else you can think of that should be notified.

I made up a box of some odds and ends before I left camp that I didn't want to carry with me and brother Gruseck is going to mail it to you. I sent my knife, my boots, seven rolls of film, my photo album and also a little yellow book for you to study. On second thought, I don't think you had better open it in the presence of the kids.

Well darling, have you regained your senses yet? I haven't. It's still hard to believe but it's true because I've got the orders in black and white. I love you, honey, and it won't be long before I can convince you I do!

Now, I know the scheme that is hatching in that clever little brain of yours but, no dice. I refer to you coming to meet me. Things are too uncertain as to where I'll land. One of our boys went home to be discharged for being over 42 and he landed in Virginia and was discharged seven days after he landed. So, there isn't much use trying to plan a meeting anywhere but Atterbury where I'll get out. In the meantime, I guess you had better hit Garceau up for a thousand dollar raise. We'll sure need a pile of rupees.

Speaking of money, that is another problem. You know me, if I haven't got plenty of money along whenever I do anything it worries me. That is my trouble now. You know I had the allotments changed in order to put it into effect July 1st. So, I had to be redlined. In other words, I didn't get paid August 1st for July. So, now I'm short. Gruseck said I can get paid for July at my new camp. But, for July, instead of you getting the regular forty dollars for the month you'll get the forty plus another fifty dollars which is the new allotment. So, even though I can get July's pay, it won't help much because it won't be over twenty-two dollars. I have about ninety dollars on me. Now, if I knew I was leaving right away it would be O.K. But, if I have to stay around camp three or four weeks I'm damn sure not going to eat GI chow when I can go into Calcutta and eat shrimp.

So, honey, when I hit the States you can probably look for a wire for money. I hate to think of doing it, I've never had to wire for money since I've been in the Army.

Darling, now about the party, oh me, I get tipsy just thinking about it. That was my first and only drunk in India and my second drunk in the Army. Not bad.

Anyhow, Nels, Johnnie, Gruseck, Hackett and several more fellows were sitting around talking. I had nineteen beers left on my card so I bought the drinks then Hackett went over to the PX and talked them out of two cases. So, we had to get a tub and some ice meanwhile guys were coming and going all the time. One of the cooks got some baked ham and bread so we didn't have to stop and go to the mess hall to eat supper. In the meanwhile, every once and a while, someone else would dig up another case of beer. Finally, about nine o'clock the party was nearing a stalemate and we were down to our last beers. So, Capt. Browne took Whitey and went over to the officers club and got a case of beer and a quart of Gordon's Gin. Well, that lasted until there wasn't any more to be had so we adjourned for a cup of coffee that some guys needed, ahem!

After that nothing would do but for all of us to take showers. I had my shower and reached over to put my on clothes so I leaned up against the wall, soaking wet, and I'll be damned if I didn't lean right up against a light switch that had the protective cover broken off. I nearly electrocuted myself. Then we went to bed. I was the first one up this morning at 5:30, I had a slight headache but that's all. Then, Gruseck, Hackett, Hammond, White and Swiheart went to the station with me and I left at eight.

Oh yes, when I was taking your pictures out from under the glass, Nels and Johnnie each took one of those latest proofs you sent. I think I should start getting jealous.

You should have seen me darling I was sitting on the edge of my bed all night long with just my shorts on. My pants were hanging on my mosquito net rack right alongside of me. I sat there like a street car conductor. All evening long, guys would come in and give me a slip of paper with a name on it to call when I get back in the States. So, I'd just reach up and stuff it in my pants pocket. This morning I went to dress and I had a pocket full of addresses and I don't know which is which. Oh me!

Well darling, guess I'd better close before this letter gets too heavy to go by air. Oh yes, don't forget to make a reservation for us at the closing dance at Westlake.

Bye for now, I love you. See you soon.

Always your

Jimmie[1]

40

Around the World

I don't know what day my father left India. It was probably soon after the Japanese broadcast their surrender on August 14, 1945. He probably spent a few days in Kanchrapara, forty-five miles north of Calcutta, waiting in one of the camps before embarking on a troop transport in the third week of August. His trip home, the final leg in his circumnavigation of the globe, took him down the muddy Hooghly River and through the wide silt delta of the Ganges to the Bay of Bengal. From there they stopped for fuel and water at the British naval base near Trincomalee, Sri Lanka, at the time known as Ceylon. Following the island's coastline clockwise for another 300 miles, the ship then struck a northwesterly course into the Arabian Sea. Two thousand miles later Jim sailed past the barren island of Socotra and entered the Gulf of Aden. Once past the narrow channel at Bab-el-Mandeb, Gate of Tears, he crossed into the Red Sea. He steamed 1,400 miles on a steady northwesterly course heading past Mecca's port of Jeddah and finally to the Gulf of Suez. There, at the Port of Suez, the ship anchored and sent a tender ashore for mail.

The trip up the gulf and through the canal was nearly 300 miles of desert sightseeing until he reached Port Said and the southeastern shores of the Mediterranean. From there, 400 miles on, the ship passed less than a hundred miles south of Crete and in so doing crossed the invisible "Welcome home" line of Western civilization.

The westward passage through the Mediterranean took him between Malta and Sicily, then along the northern shore of Tunisia, past Sardinia, and along the coasts of Algeria and Morocco. On the starboard side he had a good view of Gibraltar, then Tarifa, Spain. The bleached white lighthouse on the rocky cliffs of Cabo St. Vincent in Portugal was his last chance to photograph Europe.

From there the ship struck a westerly heading across the Atlantic for nearly 4,000 miles. The next landfall was Nantucket Island before a slow approach down Long Island. Somewhere near the mouth of the Hudson River the ship took on a pilot before negotiating the crowded channel past the Statue of Liberty to New York Harbor. Some GIs returning from India disembarked at Norfolk, Virginia. All of the returning railroad battalions used the New York port of entry.

From New York's Penn Station, Jim took a passenger train to Camp Atterbury, forty miles south of Indianapolis, a familiar place. Forty-eight hours later, on September 23, with a shine on his shoes and his mustering-out pay in the pocket of his dress uniform—the only military clothing he was allowed to keep—he stood before a colonel who handed him his discharge papers and told him, "Good luck, Hantzis."

To this the smiling former staff sergeant returned a snappy salute and replied, "Thank you, Sir."

Civilian Hantzis walked to the visitors' center at the post gate, where Marilou was waiting. The sun was warm and the sky crystal blue. It was a good day to be alive and a good day to finally be home. Walking to their 1940 Ford convertible, their arms around one another, they would have made a wonderful photograph.

Marilou said, "I brought along a surprise."

As Jim looked over at Marilou a bit puzzled, he heard their German Shepherd, Tippy, woofing a throaty welcome from behind the partially rolled-down window of their Ford.

41

Departure

The men of the 721st discontinued operations of the Bengal and Assam Railway on October 1, 1945. They were more than ready to go home to friends and family but just as ready to escape the morale-draining, hot, wet, bug-infested, miserable home they had endured for the past twenty-two months. There was no languid reminiscing about the good old days or fond remembrances brought to mind. Everybody just wanted to get the hell out of there. For ten days nearly 600 American soldier railroaders packed their duffle bags with personal belongings and war souvenirs. When everything was crated, tied-down, blocked, inventoried, and numbered, they made ready to climb aboard an Indian-crewed passenger train bound for Kanchrapara to await transport home. They departed as they came: by train.

As the U.S. railway battalions shut down their operations the last function they returned to the Indians was that of supervising train movement. The Americans were leaving behind a vastly improved railroad, a modern communications system, and tons of new equipment, some of it in use to this very day. And they were leaving behind something even more valuable.

The Americans had hired thousands of native laborers to construct the Ledo Road, redesign railroad yards, lay new track, build airfields, and toil in the manual work of war. Often illiterate and desperately poor, their ranks included Mahrattas, Madrasis, Bengalis, and Hindu and Muslim Punjabis. From the hill folk and tribes they hired Chamars, Oryias, Bihari aborigines, Garos, Nepalese, and Gurkhas. The diverse workforce prompted an anonymous wisenheimer to describe it as "an anthropologist's dream but a mess sergeant's nightmare."[1] Still, the sole fact that these very different people worked together and accomplished tasks of great importance and feats of technical difficulty was an invaluable object lesson.

The Americans served as an example to the thousands of young Indians who worked in the American-run shops, depots, and offices. The Americans relished hands-on work and were unafraid of manual labor, seeing in it no dishonor whatsoever. The GIs' freewheeling social democracy proved that a society need not be stuck in the medieval past. The American fascination with technical improvements, machinery, and the work process, from the highest ranks to the lowest, provided a model of innovation and progress. To the Indians, Americans were as wealthy as lords, but their success came from their own initiative, not from inherited privilege or social caste.

. . .

The five railroad battalions had been told they would probably be home by Thanksgiving but definitely by Christmas. Most of the 721st made it in time to share in the Thanksgiving turkey, as did the 725th and the 745th. But the 726th and 748th missed the bird by two days and didn't arrive in New York until November 24, 1945.

42

Christmas 1945

The way home had been found by all, and the heart of every man rejoiced. George Lee was back in Kansas, Alvin Carder in West Virginia, Stew White in California, Herb Witt in Wisconsin. E. O. Woods, Don Blair, Lyle Sanderson, and Rocky Agrusti were back in New York. Johnny Hammond was back in Maryland, Les Gruseck was back in Ohio, and Nels Whittaker and Jim Hantzis were back in Indiana. The paths of their lives would cross again only because of their dedication to remembering.

When the young railroaders returned to their families at Christmas 1945, they came back changed men. Jim went back to work for the New York Central Railroad as soon as he returned to Indianapolis in late September. All the other men went back to work on their respective railroads as well. Most stayed in those jobs for their entire working lives, and a good number became officers in their unions.

My father worked for the railroad until 1950, a year after I was born, then became an experimental machinist for Detroit Diesel Allison, a division of General Motors, now owned by Rolls-Royce. He worked there until he died in April 1976, eighteen months after my mother passed away. Both died entirely too young. They were hard-working, straight-laced people who deserved to enjoy the fruits of their labors, but their fates were unkind.

Years later I tried to drag from each man of the 721st his assessment of how the war had changed them. A few looked away blankly when I asked the question. Others spoke of their visceral realization that, in some cultures at some times, life is cheap. Others simply said that they were young and hesitated to sound off about their experiences.

One man, a locomotive engineer, told me that his time in the service had made him a quick study of other men. Railroading alone will do that, but railroading in a war zone no doubt intensified his survival response. "You learned to size up other guys so that you knew who you could count on and who was a bullshitter," he said. That bit of wisdom, although far from profound or original, nevertheless stuck with me throughout my writing. My own father, a man of whom I never asked the question, sized up other men—including his sons—with speed and deftness. He was a hard man to fool, and believe me, we tried.

Slowly, over my years of writing, what began as curiosity about the 721st Railway Operating Battalion grew into profound admiration. Today that admiration lives in full career as inspiration. My notions have journeyed beyond simple respect for the men's mastery of material circumstances. They had a job to do and they did it—simple, right? But the magnitude of their work leaves an abiding deference somewhere very near my heart. The men of the 721st were plucked from comfortable private lives and ordered to travel halfway around the world, take over and operate a foreign enterprise, multiply its capacity many-fold, and do it all in a time of war. Then they safely completed their circumnavigation and returned home to family and friends. On lesser plots are legends born.

Notes

1. SS *Mariposa*

1. James Hantzis to Marilou Hantzis, January 9, 1944. All family letters are in the author's possession.

2. Kaufman, "The 748th Railway Operating Battalion," 12.

3. James Hantzis to Marilou Hantzis, January 9, 1944.

4. Marilou Hantzis to James Hantzis, October 22, 1944, and June 13, 1945.

5. Romanus and Sunderland, *Stilwell's Mission to China*, 363.

2. Leaving Bombay

1. Dunn, "The Ledo Road," 327.

2. C. N. Trueman, "The Civil War in China 1945 to 1949," History Learning Site, May 26, 2015, http://www.historylearningsite.co.uk/china_war.htm.

3. "Douglas C-47/DC-3 'Cheeky Charley,'" Pacific Aviation Museum, May 7, 2012, http://www.pacificaviationmuseum.org/pearl-harbor-blog/douglas-c-47dc-3-cheeky-charlie-7.

4. Alden Whitman, "The Life of Chiang Kai-shek," *New York Times*, April 6, 1975, http://www.nytimes.com/learning/general/onthisday/bday/1031.html.

3. Indian Rails

1. V. Sridhar, "Chronicle of a Strike," review of *The Indian Railways Strike of 1974*, by Stephen Sherlock, *Frontline* 18, no. 19 (2001), http://www.frontline.in/static/html/fl1819/18190750.htm.

2. *Railway Times*, May 1859, 533.

3. *Railway Times*, May 1859, 533.

4. Verne, *Around the World in 80 Days*, 61.

5. "Chronology of Railways in India, Part 3 (1900–1947)," Indian Railways Fan Club, accessed June 12, 2008, http://irfca.org/faq/faq-history3.html.

6. Smith, "The Archaeology of Food Preference," 486.

7. Smith, "The Archaeology of Food Preference," 480.

8. Padmanabhan, "The Great Bengal Famine," 11–24.

9. Tully, "India and the Second World War." Tully cites three million deaths.

10. Gideon Polya, "The Forgotten Holocaust—The 1943/44 Bengal Famine," *Global Avoidable Mortality* (blog), July 11, 2005, http://globalavoidablemortality.blogspot.com/2005/07/forgotten-holocaust-194344-bengal.html.

11. Bhatia, *Famines in India*.

4. To Parbatipur

1. An *anna* was one-sixteenth of a rupee, worth a pittance. My father kept only five dollars of his monthly pay and sent the rest home.

6. The Ledo Road

1. Romanus and Sunderland, *Stilwell's Mission to China*, 77.
2. Romanus and Sunderland, *Stilwell's Mission to China*, 247.
3. Dunn, "The Ledo Road," 300.
4. Romanus and Sunderland, *Stilwell's Mission to China*, 306.
5. Dunn, "The Ledo Road," 330.
6. Dunn, "The Ledo Road," 332.
7. Romanus and Sunderland, *Stilwell's Mission to China*, 348.
8. Romanus and Sunderland, *Stilwell's Mission to China*, 350.
9. Dunn, "The Ledo Road," 336.

7. Relay

1. Romanus and Sunderland, *Stilwell's Mission to China*, 359.
2. Romanus and Sunderland, *Stilwell's Mission to China*, 362.
3. Romanus and Sunderland, *Stilwell's Mission to China*, 362.
4. Bykofsky and Larson, *The Transportation Corps*, 552.
5. Bykofsky and Larson, *The Transportation Corps*, 552.
6. Gray, *Railroading in Eighteen Countries*, 270.
7. Romanus and Sunderland, *Stilwell's Mission to China*, 363.

9. Inside the 721st

1. Kaufman, "The 748th Railway Operating Battalion," 11.
2. Gray, *Railroading in Eighteen Countries*, 275.

10. Merrill's Marauders

1. Center of Military History, *Merrill's Marauders*, 14.
2. Center of Military History, *Merrill's Marauders*, 8.
3. Center of Military History, *Merrill's Marauders*, 16; "Frank Merrill," *Wikipedia*, https://en.wikipedia.org/wiki/Frank_Merrill.
4. Hogan, *U.S. Army Special Operations*, 113.

11. Company B

1. Kirby, *The War against Japan*, 3: 506.

12. Fire

1. "Examples of Japanese Propaganda Dropped into Burma from 1942 to 1945," Burma Star Association, accessed September 7, 2016, http://www.burmastar.org.uk/burma-campaign/japanese-propaganda/.
2. "Examples of Japanese Propaganda Dropped into Burma from 1942 to 1945."
3. O'Neill, "Secret History," 3.
4. James Hantzis to Marilou Hantzis, March 27, 1945.

13. Mutaguchi's Gift

1. Allen, *Burma*, 153.
2. Allen, *Burma*, 229.

14. The Battle of Kohima

1. Allen, *Burma*, 228.
2. Allen, *Burma*, 230.
3. Arthur Swinson, *Four Samurai* (N.p.: Hutchison, 1968), cited in Allen, *Burma*, 230.
4. Slim, *Defeat into Victory*, 271.
5. Commonwealth War Graves Commission, *The Battle of Kohima*, 9.
6. Slim, *Defeat into Victory*, 271.

16. Inbound

1. Shupe, "Transportation within the CBI—Part 1," 9.
2. "Transportation Corps Units," CBI History, last modified March 25, 2014, http://www.cbi-history.com/part_iv_trans.html#10.

17. Material Inferiority

1. Wai, "The Effect of Material Inferiority."
2. Kirby, *The War against Japan*, 3: 198.
3. Romanus and Sunderland, *Stilwell's Command Problems*, 195.
4. Allen, *Burma*, 232.
5. Commonwealth War Graves Commission, *The Battle of Kohima*, 8.
6. Wai, "The Effect of Material Inferiority."
7. Romanus and Sunderland, *Stilwell's Command Problems*, 195.
8. Commonwealth War Graves Commission, *The Battle of Kohima*, 3.
9. Slim, *Defeat into Victory*, 337. Said Lieutenant-General Slim of the Japanese soldiers sent against his 14th Army, "There can be no question of the supreme courage and hardihood of the Japanese soldiers. . . . I know of no army that could have equaled them" (337).

19. The Siege of Myitkyina

1. Slim, *Defeat into Victory*, 134.
2. Hogan, *U.S. Army Special Operations*, 117.
3. Romanus and Sunderland, *Stilwell's Command Problems*, 223.
4. Center of Military History, *Merrill's Marauders*, 98.
5. Romanus and Sunderland, *Stilwell's Command Problems*, 242.
6. Romanus and Sunderland, *Stilwell's Command Problems*, 238.
7. "H&S Company History and Roster," 16. Also see Sinclair, "Running on Time in a Timeless Land," 42.
8. Kaufman, "The 748th Railway Operating Battalion," 17.

21. Kaunia Junction

1. The railroad is divided into blocks. The person in charge of a block is called

the station master or operator. "Second trick" means second shift, usually the shift that starts in early afternoon. Third trick starts around 10:30 p.m. to midnight.

23. Japanese Retrench
1. MacGarrigle, *Central Burma*, 7.

25. Stepping Up
1. Edgar Laytha, "Military Railroaders In India," *CBI Roundup*, Delhi, November 9, 1944, accessed September 7, 2016, http://www.cbi-theater.com/roundup /roundup110944.html.
2. Sinclair, "Running on Time in a Timeless Land," 41.
3. O'Neill, "Secret History," 3. The figures cited in this section are taken from a document authored for the battalion's commanding officer.

27. Milepost 103
1. Romanus and Sunderland, *Time Runs Out in CBI*, 314.
2. Romanus and Sunderland, *Time Runs Out in CBI*, 318.
3. Romanus and Sunderland, *Time Runs Out in CBI*, 348.
4. For background on African American troop activity in the China-Burma-India theater, see the three volumes by Romanus and Sunderland.
5. Sinclair, "Confusion beyond Imagination."
6. Anders, *The Ledo Road*.
7. Dunn, "The Ledo Road," 337.
8. Romanus and Sunderland, *Time Runs Out in CBI*, 136.

28. The Road Less Traveled
1. Anders, *The Ledo Road*, 206.
2. Romanus and Sunderland, *Time Runs Out in CBI*, 141.
3. Sinclair, "Confusion beyond Imagination," 11.
4. Anders, *The Ledo Road*, 208.
5. Sinclair, "Confusion beyond Imagination."
6. Romanus and Sunderland, *Time Runs Out in CBI*, 141.
7. *Holocaust Encyclopedia*, s.v. "Liberation of Nazi Camps," last modified July 2, 2016, http://www.ushmm.org/wlc/article.php?lang=en&ModuleId=10005131.
8. Knell, *To Destroy a City*, 254.
9. USAF, Historical Division, Research Studies Institute, Air University, "Historical Analysis of the 14–15 February 1945 Bombings of Dresden," 1945, accessed September 7, 2016, http://www.afhso.af.mil/shared/media/document /AFD-110208-030.pdf, par. 3.
10. *Encyclopedia Britannica Online*, s.v. "Dresden," accessed September 8, 2016, https://www.britannica.com/place/Dresden-Germany.
11. U.S. Department of Energy, Office of History & Heritage Resources, "First Steps toward International Control, (1941–July 1945)," accessed September 7, 2016, https://www.osti.gov/opennet/manhattan-project-history /Events/1945-present/international_control_1.htm.

12. *New York Times*, "President Roosevelt's Report to Congress on the Crimea Conference," March 1, 1945, http://www.ibiblio.org/pha/policy/1945/450301a.html.

29. Toy Train to Shangri-La
1. "H&S Company History and Roster," 17.
2. Twain, *Following the Equator*, 348.
3. James Hantzis to Marilou Hantzis, January 10, 1945.

30. Crossing Irrawaddy
1. Allen, *Burma*, 391.
2. Slim, *Defeat into Victory*, 314.
3. Slim, *Defeat into Victory*, 316.
4. Allen, *Burma*, 393.
5. Anders, *The Ledo Road*, 5.
6. Allen, *Burma*, 393.
7. Slim, *Defeat into Victory*, 317.
8. Allen, *Burma*, 398.
9. Slim, *Defeat into Victory*, 317.
10. Slim, *Defeat into Victory*, 316.
11. Slim, *Defeat into Victory*, 368.
12. Slim, *Defeat into Victory*, 384, 369.
13. *Encyclopedia Britannica Online*, s.v. "Irrawaddy," accessed September 8, 2016, https://www.britannica.com/place/Irrawaddy-River.
14. Allen, *Burma*, 394.
15. Slim, *Defeat into Victory*, 371.
16. Slim, *Defeat into Victory*, 374.
17. Slim, *Defeat into Victory*, 375.
18. *Encyclopedia Britannica Online*, s. v. "Meiktila," accessed September 8, 2016, https://www.britannica.com/place/Meiktila.
19. Slim, *Defeat into Victory*, 375.
20. Slim, *Defeat into Victory*, 385.
21. Slim, *Defeat into Victory*, 385.
22. *Encyclopedia Britannica Online*, s.v. "Mandalay," accessed September 8, 2016, https://www.britannica.com/place/Mandalay-Myanmar.
23. Slim, *Defeat into Victory*, 386.
24. Slim, *Defeat into Victory*, 389.
25. Slim, *Defeat into Victory*, 390.
26. Slim, *Defeat into Victory*, 392.
27. Slim, *Defeat into Victory*, 394.

31. The Home Fires
1. Memo, "Reclassification of Impregnite, Shoe, M1," to Chairman, Chemical Warfare Technical Committee, December 25, 1946, http://www.dtic.mil/dtic/tr/fulltext/u2/a544845.pdf.

32. Blue Flag

1. "Indian Elephant Causes Engine Failure," *Central Headlight* (New York Central Railroad), ca. June 1944. The following engine failure story was sent to F. K. Mitchell, assistant general superintendent, New York, by Maj. F. H. Winget, formerly general foreman, Shelby Street Engine House, Indianapolis, then with a Railway Operating Battalion on the Bengal & Assam Railroad, India.

34. The New President

1. Giangreco, "Casualty Projections for U.S. Invasions of Japan."
2. Giangreco, "Casualty Projections for U.S. Invasions of Japan."
3. Giangreco, "Casualty Projections for U.S. Invasions of Japan."
4. "H&S Company History and Roster," 17.
5. Romanus and Sunderland, *Time Runs Out in CBI*, 313.
6. "721st ROB Company B History," 18.
7. "721st ROB Company B History," 18.

35. Endgame

1. "Rangoon—End & Beginning," *Time* online, May 14, 1945, accessed September 8, 2016, http://content.time.com/time/subscriber/article/0,33009,792085,00.html. Rangoon is a corruption of Yan Kon; it was so named by a conquering Burmese king in 1753.
2. Slim, *Defeat into Victory*, 396.
3. Slim, *Defeat into Victory*, 396.
4. Slim, *Defeat into Victory*, 400.
5. Slim, *Defeat into Victory*, 401, 400.
6. Allen, *Burma*, 460.
7. Slim, *Defeat into Victory*, 405.
8. Slim, *Defeat into Victory*, 407.
9. Allen, *Burma*, 465.
10. Slim, *Defeat into Victory*, 408.
11. Slim, *Defeat into Victory*, 408, 496.

36. Above Rangoon Jail

1. This dialogue is imagined, based on the accounts in Slim, *Defeat into Victory*; Allen, *Burma*.
2. Slim, *Defeat into Victory*, 418. Also see "Rifleman Leslie Spoors," Pegasus Archive, accessed June 16, 2008, http://www.pegasusarchive.org/pow/leslie_spoors.htm.
3. "Rifleman Leslie Spoors."
4. "Rifleman Leslie Spoors."
5. Slim, *Defeat into Victory*, 420.
6. Slim, *Defeat into Victory*, 422.
7. Slim, *Defeat into Victory*, 428.
8. Slim, *Defeat into Victory*, 429.

9. Slim, *Defeat into Victory*, 436.

10. *Jungle Battle Burma* (New York: A&E Television Networks, 2001), video.

37. Germany Surrenders

1. Harry S. Truman Library and Museum, "Broadcast to the American People Announcing the Surrender of Germany, May 8, 1945," https://www.truman library.org/ww2/veday.htm.

2. Marilou Hantzis to James Hantzis, October 2, 1944; "George J. Garceau, M.D. 1896–1977," *Journal of Joint and Bone Surgery* 61, no. 5 (1979): 793, http://jbjs.org/content/61/5/793.

3. Marilou Hantzis to James Hantzis, May 25, 1945.

38. Discharge

1. "The Armistice Agreement with Bulgaria: October 28, 1944," Avalon Project at Yale Law School, accessed June 16, 2008, http://www.yale.edu/lawweb /avalon/wwii/bulgaria.htm.

39. The Conductor

1. James Hantzis to Marilou Hantzis, August 13, 1945.

41. Departure

1. Romanus and Sunderland, *Time Runs Out in CBI*, 300.

Bibliography

Manuscripts and Archives

Goodman, Chad W. "It Was Our Job, No One Complained: A Young World War II Soldier's Life." Unpublished manuscript in author's possession.

"H&S Company History and Roster." Headquarters and Service Company, 721st Railway Operating Battalion. Unpublished manuscript in author's possession.

Kaye (Komorowski), Matthew. "Scout Trip to India." Unpublished manuscript in author's possession.

O'Neill, R. B. "Secret History: 721st ROB, 1944." Unpublished manuscript in author's possession.

"721st ROB Company B History." Unpublished manuscript in author's possession.

Skrentny, John C. "Trip Home from Calcutta 1945." Unpublished manuscript in author's possession.

Stapf, Joseph. "History of the 721st Railway Operating Battalion 1943–1945 India." Unpublished manuscript in author's possession.

Published Works

Adamczyk, Richard D., and Morris J. MacGregor, eds. *United States Army in World War II: Readers Guide.* Washington DC: Center for Military History, U.S. Army, 1992.

Air Operations in China-Burma-India World War II. Washington DC: U.S. Strategic Bombing Survey, Military Analysis Division, 1947.

Allen, Louis. *Burma: The Longest War 1941-45.* London: Phoenix Press, 1984.

Anders, Leslie. *The Ledo Road: General Joseph W. Stilwell's Highway to China.* Norman: University of Oklahoma Press, 1965.

Astor, Gerald. *The Jungle War: Mavericks, Marauders, and Madmen in the China-Burma-India Theater of World War II.* Hoboken NJ: John Wiley, 2004.

Ayer, Hugh M. "Hoosier Labor in Second World War." *Indiana Magazine of History,* June 1963.

Ball, Don, Jr. *Portrait of the Rails.* New York: Galahad Books, 1972.

Barker, Oscar. "History of the 721st." *Troy Record,* May 9, 1978.

Beech Grove Public Library. *Working in the Beech Grove Shops: An Oral History.* Beech Grove IN: Beech Grove Public Library, 1998.

Belden, Jack. *Retreat with Stilwell.* New York: Knopf, 1943.

Bengal and Assam Railway. *Working Time Table No. 164 Metre Gauge Parbati- pur and Lalmanirhat Divisions.* Calcutta: East Indian Railway Press, 1944.

Bhatia, B. M. *Famines in India: A Study in Some Aspects of the Economic His- tory of India with Special Reference to Food Problem.* Delhi: Konark, 1985.

Bjorge, Gary J. *Merrill's Marauders: Combined Operations in Northern Burma in 1944.* Washington DC: U.S. Army Center of Military History, 1996.

Bodenhamer, David, and Robert G. Barrows, eds. *Encyclopedia of Indianapo- lis.* Bloomington: Indiana University Press, 1994.

Briscoe, C. H. "Kachin Rangers: Allied Guerrillas in World War II Burma." Fort Bragg NC: John F. Kennedy Special Warfare Center and School, 2002.

British Railways Press Office. *Facts about British Railways in Wartime 1943.* Lon- don: Baynard Press, 1943.

Browne, Gordon. "We Took a Hell of a Beating: General 'Vinegar Joe' Stilwell in Burma." *Infantry Magazine,* May–August 2000.

Budrow, Roger. "NYC to Spend 3 1/2 Million Here." *Indianapolis News,* Octo- ber 12, 1948.

Burlington 745th Railway Operating Battalion Association. "History of the Battalion." N.p.: n.d.

Burnes, Brian. "Slow Roads." *Kansas City Star,* July 26, 1995.

Bykofsky, Joseph, and Harold Larson. *The Transportation Corps: Operations Overseas.* Washington DC: Office of the Chief of Military History, Depart- ment of the Army, 1957.

Carter, E. F. *Railways in Wartime.* London: Frederick Muller, 1964.

Case, Dick. "Rocky's Collections Are Now Rocky's Museum." *Syracuse Her- ald American,* June 29, 1997.

CBI Roundup. "G.I. Railroaders Solve Problem of I-B Supply." August 2, 1945.

——. "President Amplifies the Reason for Uncle Joe's Recall." November 9, 1944.

Center of Military History, U.S. Army. *Merrill's Marauders (February–May 1944).* Washington DC: Center of Military History, U.S. Army, 1945.

Collingham, Lizzie. *The Taste of War: World War II and the Battle for Food.* Lon- don: Penguin Books, 2011.

Commonwealth War Graves Commission. *The Battle of Kohima, North East India 4 April–22 June 1944.* London: Commonwealth War Graves Com- mission and HMSO, 2004.

DeNevi, Don. *America's Fighting Railroads.* Missoula MT: Pictorial Histories, 1996.

DeNevi, Don, and Bob Hall. *United States Military Railway Service: America's Soldier-Railroaders in WWII.* Boston: Boston Mills Press, 1991.

Deutschman, Paul E. "Four Marauders." *Life,* March 15, 1948.

Dunn, James W. "The Ledo Road." In *Builders and Fighters: U.S. Army Engi- neers in World War II,* ed. Barry W. Fowle. Publication No. EP 870-1-42. Washington DC: Office of History, U.S. Army Corps of Engineers, 1992.

https://ia800308.us.archive.org/17/items/BuildersAndFighters/Build
ersAndFighters_text.pdf.

Dwyer, John B. *Scouts and Raiders: The Navy's First Special Warfare Comman-dos*. Westport CT: Praeger, 1993.

Esarey, Logan. *History of Indiana from Its Exploration to 1850*. Indianapolis: Hoosier Heritage Press, 1970.

Farris, Bain J. *St. Vincent Hospital and Health Care Center, Inc.: Past, Present and Future*. New York: Newcomen Society of the United States, 1988.

Fenby, Jonathan. *Chiang Kai-Shek: China's Generalissimo and the Nation He Lost*. New York: Carroll and Graf, 2003.

Forty, George. *British Army Handbook 1939–1945*. Stroud, UK: Sutton, 1998.

———. *U.S. Army Handbook 1939–1945*. Stroud, UK: Sutton, 2003.

Giangreco, D. M. "Casualty Projections for the U.S. Invasions of Japan, 1945–1946: Planning and Policy Implications." *Journal of Military History* 61 (July 1997): 521–82. http://theamericanpresident.us/images/projections.pdf.

———. "Operation Downfall: The Devil Was in the Details." *Joint Force Quarterly*, Autumn 1995.

Glines, Carroll V. *Attack on Yamamoto*. Atglen PA: Schiffer Military House, 1993.

Gray, Carl R., Jr. *Railroading in Eighteen Countries*. New York: Charles Scribner's Sons, 1955.

Griffo, Charles. "Army Travel Policy Rapped: City Plays Vital War Role." *Indianapolis Star*, July 22, 1945.

———. "Indiana—World War, 1939–1945." *Indianapolis Star*, November 5, 1945.

Hartmann, Susan M. "Women, War, and the Limits of Change." *National Forum*, September 22, 1995.

Hogan, David W. *India-Burma: The United States Army Campaigns of World War II*. Washington DC: Center for Military History, U.S. Army.

Hogan, David W., Jr. *U.S. Army Special Operations in World War II*. Washington DC: Office of the Chief of Military History, Department of the Army, 1992.

Holmes, Richard. *Acts of War: The Behavior of Men in Battle*. New York: Free Press, 1985.

Horn, Bernd. "Strength Born from Weakness: The Establishment of the Raiding Concept and the British Commandos." *Canadian Military Journal*, Autumn 2005.

Hottelet, Richard C. "Why Stalin Rushed In: The Fall of Berlin 1945." *New Leader*, May 1, 2002.

Indianapolis News. "Avon Yard to Bar Russ Rail Experts." December 1, 1960.

———. "Beech Grove to Do NYC Diesel Work." September 1, 1954.

———. "Indiana Nurses to Register for Defense Plan Inventory." February 6, 1941.

———. "New York Central Buys 2,460 Acres." March 14, 1906.

Indianapolis Star. "All Railroads Operating Here Plagued by Man Power Shortage." March 25, 1945.

———. "Big 4 Yards Keep City on Rail Map." January 11, 1961.

———. "Hoosier Railroad Workers Join Walkout: Few Trains Move Here." May 24, 1946.

———. "Industrial Map Shows Indianapolis Hub of Great Future Inland Empire." December 16, 1918.

———. "Work on Multimillion-Dollar Rail Freight Yard to Begin Monday." May 29, 1959.

Indianapolis Star Magazine. "The Big Switch." June 5, 1983.

Indian State Railways. *General Rules of Indian State Railways, Part I*. Calcutta: East Indian Railway Press, 1944.

Iriye, Akira. *The Origins of the Second World War in Asia and the Pacific*. London: Longman, 1987.

Kamat, Jytotsna. "Netaji Subhas Chandra Bose." *Kamat's Potpourri*, January 26, 1999.

Kaufman, Dave. "The 725th Railway Operating Battalion." Insigne.org, 1995. http://www.insigne.org/725ROB-I.htm.

———. "The 748th Railway Operating Battalion." *Trading Post*, October–December 1999.

Kessler, Lloyd L. "To Open the Ledo Road in Burma during World War II, U.S. Combat Engineers Did More Than Just Build." *World War II Magazine*, March 2001.

Kirby, S. Woodburn. *The War against Japan*. Vol. 2: *India's Most Dangerous Hour*. New Delhi: Natraj, 1989.

———. *The War against Japan*. Vol. 3: *The Decisive Battles*. London: HMSO, 1960.

Knell, Hermann. *To Destroy a City: Strategic Bombing and Its Human Consequences in World War II*. New York: Da Capo, 2003.

Kraus, Theresa L. *China Offensive 5 May–2 September 1945*. Washington DC: Center for Military History, U.S. Army, 2003.

Lee, Ulysses. *The Employment of Negro Troops*. Publication No. 11-4. Washington DC: Center for Military History, U.S. Army, 2000.

Levin, Ruben. "Yank Railmen Win Glory." *Machinists' Monthly Journal*, September 1944.

Life. "Merrill's Marauders." June 1944.

Liljestrand, Robert A., and David R. Sweetland. *Freight Equipment of the New York Central*. Hanover PA: Railroad Press, 2001.

London Gazette. "Air Operations in South East Asia from 1st June, 1944, to the Occupation of Rangoon, 2nd May, 1945." April 6, 1951, third supplement.

MacGarrigle, George L. *Central Burma: The United States Army Campaigns of World War II*. Washington DC: U.S. Army Center of Military History, n.d.

Maitra, Ramtanu, and Susan Maitra. "Northeast India: Target of British Apartheid." *Executive Intelligence Review* 22, no. 41 (1995). http://www.larouchepub.com/other/1995/2241_ne_india_history.html.

McCord, Al. "Indianapolis Was Railroad City." *Indianapolis Star*, November 7, 1971.

"Metre-Gauge R.R. Is Mighty War Weapon." [*CBI Roundup?*]. N.p.: n.d.

Metz, Mark. "Training of Railway Operating Battalions and Railway Shop Battalions—Camp Claiborne, LA." *Army Transportation Museum Foundation Newsletter* 26, no. 1 (2011).

Miller, Russell. *Behind the Line: The Oral History of Special Operations in World War II.* New York: St. Martin's Press, 2002.

Natsios, Andrew, and Melita Leoussis. "The Politics of Famine." *Odyssey*, November–December 2008.

Newell, Clayton R. *Burma, 1942: The United States Army Campaigns of World War II.* Washington DC: U.S. Army Center of Military History, n.d.

NYC Central Headlight. "American Soldiers Operate Strategic India-Burma Lines." N.d., ca. 1944.

Ogburn, Charlton, Jr. *The Marauders.* New York: Harper and Brothers, 1956.

Padmanabhan, S. Y. "The Great Bengal Famine." *Annual Review of Phytopathology* 11 (September 1973): 11–24.

Patrick, Corbin. "City Served by 184 Trains Daily in '09." *Indianapolis Star*, April 26, 1959.

Phoenix (An Allied Magazine for All Allied Forces in South East Asia Command). "LofC." June 2, 1945.

Quartermaster Review. "Supplies for the Troops in Burma," May–June 1944.

Railway Times. "India—Revolts and Railways," October 10, 1857.

Rehagen, Tony. "On Duty: A Sailor's Story." *Indianapolis Monthly*, September 2005.

Richardson, Dave. "Northern Burma." *Yank*, March 17, 1945, China-Burma-India edition.

Riter, W. F. "Rail Transportation; An Historical Military Study." *Quartermaster Review*, March–April 1927.

Romanus, Charles F., and Riley Sunderland. *United States Army in World War II: China-Burma-India Theater. Stilwell's Command Problems.* Washington DC: Center for Military History, U.S. Army, 1987.

Romanus, Charles F., and Riley Sunderland. *United States Army in World War II: China-Burma-India Theater. Stilwell's Mission to China.* Washington DC: Office of the Chief of Military History, Department of the Army, 1987.

Romanus, Charles F., and Riley Sunderland. *United States Army in World War II: China-Burma-India Theater. Time Runs Out in CBI.* Washington DC: Center for Military History, U.S. Army, 1999.

Shaw, Alan. "Marching on to Laffan's Plain—Chapter 1." BBC. October 24, 2004. http://www.bbc.co.uk/history/ww2peopleswar/categories /c55075/.

Sherry, Mark D. *China Defensive 1942–1945.* Washington DC: Center for Military History, U.S. Army, 2003.

Shupe, Joseph B. "Transportation in the CBI (Four Parts)." *CBI Roundup*, Fall 1996–Summer 1998.

———. "Transportation within the CBI—Part I." *CBIVA Sound-Off*, Fall 1996. http://www.cbi-theater.com/soundoff/CBI_VI_157-187.pdf.

———. "Transportation within the CBI—Part 3: The Assam Line of Communications (LOC)." *CBIVA Sound-Off*, Winter 1998.

Simons, Richard S., and Frank H. Parker. *Railroads of Indiana*. Bloomington: Indiana University Press, 1997.

Sinclair, William Boyd. "Confusion beyond Imagination." *Ex-CBI Roundup*, June–July 1989. http://www.cbi-theater.com/ledoroad/Story_firstconvoy.html.

———. "Running on Time in a Timeless Land." *Ex-CBI Roundup*, November 1950. http://www.cbi-history.com/part_vi_ba_railway2.html.

Slim, Sir William. *Defeat into Victory*. New York: David McKay, 1961.

Smith, Monica. "The Archaeology of Food Preference." *American Anthropologist* 108, no. 3 (2006): 480–93.

Smith, W. H. B. *Small Arms of the World*. 5th ed. Harrisburg PA: Military Service, 1955.

Stanton, Shelby L. *World War II Order of Battle*. New York: Galahad Books, 1984.

Stone, James H. *Crisis Fleeting: Original Reports on Military Medicine in India and Burma in the Second World War*. Washington DC: Office of the Surgeon General, Department of the Army, 1969.

Stover, John F. *American Railroads*. Chicago: University of Chicago Press, 1961.

Swanson, Douglas J. "Reporting on a Wartime Social Experience: Heroes, Hooligans, and the Zoot Suit Riots." Paper presented at the 41st Annual Conference of the Western Social Science Association, Fort Worth TX, April 23, 1999.

Terkel, Studs. "One Hell of a Big Bang." *Guardian* (London), August 6, 2002.

The Old Gray Major [pseud.]. "Malaria . . . and a Railroad." *Ex-CBI Roundup*, November 1961.

Theroux, Paul. "Across the Indian Subcontinent." *National Geographic*, June 1984.

Time. "Rangoon—End and Beginning." May 14, 1945.

Toll, Ian W. "A Reluctant Enemy." *New York Times*, December 6, 2011.

Tuchman, Barbara W. *Stilwell and the American Experience in China*. New York: Grove Press, 1970.

Tully, Mark. "India and the Second World War: The Army History Forgot." *Independent* (London), June 3, 2005.

Twain, Mark. *Following the Equator: A Journey around the World*. Hartford CT: American Publishing Company, 1897. Project Gutenberg, http://www.gutenberg.org/files/2895/2895-h/2895-h.htm.

U.S. Army. *Rail Transport in a Theater of Operations, FM 55-20*. Washington DC: U.S. Department of the Army, 2000.

———. *U.S. Army Survival Handbook*. Guilford CT: Lyons Press, 2002.

U.S. Labor Goes to War. Washington DC: War Production Board, 1942.

USS *Indianapolis* Survivors. *Only 317 Survived! Navy's Worst Tragedy at Sea . . . 880 Men Died*. Indianapolis IN: Printing Partners, 2002.

U.S. War Department. *Handbook on Japanese Military Forces*. Baton Rouge: Louisiana State University Press, 1944.

U.S. War and Navy Departments. *A Pocket Guide to India*. Washington DC: 1942.

Van Fleet, James A. *Rail Transport and the Winning of Wars*. Washington DC: Association of American Railroads, 1956.

Verne, Jules. *Around the World in 80 Days*. Paris: Routledge, 1873.

Wai, Wong Chee. "The Effect of Material Inferiority: An Analysis of Japanese Defeat in the Battle for Imphal, 1944." *Pointer: Journal of the Singapore Armed Forces* 30, no. 1 (2004). http://www.mindef.gov.sg/imindef/pub lications/pointer/journals/2004/v30n1/features/feature6.html.

Wardlow, Chester. *The Transportation Corps: Movements, Training, and Supply*. Washington DC: Center for Military History, U.S. Army, 1990.

———. *The Transportation Corps: Responsibilities, Organization and Operations*. Washington, DC: Office of the Chief of Military History, Department of the Army, 1957.

Webster, Donovan. *The Burma Road*. New York: Farrar, Straus and Giroux, 2003.

Williams, Lewis P. "Crossing the Irrawaddy prior to the xiv Army Recapture of Mandalay." BBC. November 9, 2003. http://www.bbc.co.uk/history /ww2peopleswar/stories/70/a2006470.shtml.

"Yank's Magic Carpet Ride." *Yank*, 1945, China-Burma-India edition.

Yu, Maochun. *OSS in China: Prelude to Cold War*. New Haven CT: Yale University Press, 1996.

Ziel, Ron. *Steel Rails to Victory*. New York: Hawthorne Books, 1970.

Ziemke, Earl F. "Redeployment and Readjustment." In *The U.S. Army in the Occupation of Germany 1944–1946*. Washington DC: Center of Military History U.S. Army, 1990. http://www.globalsecurity.org/military/library /report/other/us-army_germany_1944-46_ch18.htm.

Index